A Wine Lover's Guide

Acknowledgments

This book could not have been written without the helpful cooperation of winemakers, wine companies, and wine associations in all the wine-producing countries. We are very grateful to them for this support.

We would like to extend our special thanks to:
Beate Berkelmann-Löhnertz and Hartwig Holst, Geisenheim; Subhash Arora, Indian Wine Academy, DelWine, Delhi; Karishma Chandy, Sula Vineyards; Mark L. Chien, Penn State Cooperative Extension, Lancaster, PA; Karel Bush, Michigan Grape & Wine Industry Council, Lansing, MI; Kosei Ajimura, Château Mercian, Japan; Lynne Sheriff MW, London; Fabiano Maciel and Juliana Zancan, Miolo Wine Group, Brazil; Sienna Spencer-Markles, Burbank, CA.

© h.f.ullmann publishing GmbH
Original title: *Wein Guide für Kenner*
ISBN 978-3-8480-0328-0

Editing and proofreading, layout, and typesetting: Christian Heße & Martina Schlagenhaufer
Graphic design: Erill Fritz, Berlin
Project management: Isabel Weiler
Cover photograph: © h.f.ullmann publishing GmbH / Faber & Partner, Thomas Pothmann

© for the English edition: h.f.ullmann publishing GmbH

Translation from German: Ann Drummond in association with First Edition Translations Ltd; Paul Aston, Helen Atkins, Peter Barton, Anthea Bell, Susan Cox, Richard Elliott, Harriet Horsfield, Susan James, Eithne McCarthy, Michele McMeekin, Martin Pearce, Michael Scuffil, Christine Smith, and Anthony Vivis in association with Cambridge Publishing Management, Cambridge, U.K.
Editing: Robert Anderson in association with First Edition Translations Ltd
Typesetting: The Write Idea in association with First Edition Translations Ltd

Overall responsibility for production: h.f.ullmann publishing GmbH, Potsdam, Germany

Printed in Italy, 2013

ISBN 978-3-8480-0341-9

10 9 8 7 6 5 4 3 2 1
X IX VIII VII VI V IV III II I

www.ullmann-publishing.com
newsletter@ullmann-publishing.com

André Dominé (Ed.)

A Wine Lover's Guide

AUTHORS

André Dominé

Hartwig Holst

Hélène Jaeger

h.f.ullmann

8 Foreword

10 In the vineyard
Hélène Jaeger & André Dominé

72 In the winery

Hélène Jaeger & André Dominé

128 The wine-producing countries
André Dominé

214 Appendix

Foreword

If you are reading this book, you, like me, must be someone who has caught the wine bug. As a young man, I certainly enjoyed drinking wine, but it was only later that I really began to take an interest in it.

When my wife and I moved to a wine village in Roussillon, we did in fact acquire a vineyard, not so much because we loved wine, however, but to create a quiet buffer zone around our home. Anyhow, we learned how to cultivate this vineyard and became minor members of the little wine cooperative, in which everyone had to lend a hand from time to time. Then some friends of ours, a couple in publishing, asked if I would write a book about Roussillon wine for them, and my real apprenticeship in wine began in earnest, although generally the emphasis was on the practice rather than the theory.

Over a period of several months, I spent five days a week visiting winegrowing estates and wineries. I took part in regular tastings, of course, but I gained far deeper insights about wine from the winegrowers and cellar masters themselves. They took me into their vineyards, introduced me to grape varieties, and explained their working methods. They also took me along to their cellars, where they showed me the materials they work with—their presses, tanks, and temperature-control systems (a must in southern climes). I found out about yeasts, fermentation management, and skin contact times, and marveled at old tuns and new barriques.

While every winegrower did the same basic job—cultivating wine plots, vines, and grapes, maximizing the harvest and putting it into wine production—each was guided by their own personal vision and philosophy as well as by their experiences and, as a result, every wine was different. This is precisely why wine is exceptionally fascinating, as both a subject and a pleasurable activity: No other food or gastronomic luxury offers such an immense variety.

Of course, you can stick to simply enjoying the wine: After all, there are some wine critics for whom it begins and ends with tastings. I have always found it more rewarding to understand more about the wine, and how what happens in the vineyard and winery produces such diversity. This lays the groundwork for a more satisfying engagement with the whole process of winemaking, and developing a deeper understanding of winemakers' work, their passion, and their wines. In this way, our appreciation of wine takes on a new dimension. It opens up access to the wine-producing countries and regions of the world, with all their distinctive features, and provides a rewarding opportunity to explore them—glass in hand—in greater depth.

To your good health, then!
André Dominé

In the vineyard

Wine begins in the vineyard, as nearly every wine grower is now quick to tell you. This may sound fairly self-evident, but it actually represents a significant U-turn. After the wars and disasters of the first half of the 20th century, high productivity was seen as the top priority even in viticulture. Concentrated use of chemical products—from artificial fertilizers to herbicides, pesticides, fungicides, and anti-rot sprays—was a guarantee of high yields first and foremost, at the expense of healthy vines and grape crops, and great wines. As early as 1975 pioneering wine-makers recognized the effects these chemicals were having on nature, soils, and plants.

A very simple measure proved to be an eye-opener for many wine growers. Around 1990 a process of grape selection began: It gradually dawned on people that good wine could only be produced from healthy grapes. To ensure this happened, all the diseased, unripe, overripe, or damaged berries were simply weeded out—stems, stalks, leaves, weeds, other foreign bodies, and all. So simple, and yet revolutionary. From this point on, the quality of wine took a quantitative leap, and success created a precedent.

Suddenly top producers began to question all aspects of the traditional pillars written in stone, and what it had cost them, especially in terms of the level of yield and the working practices in the vineyard. In search of the perfect grape, they began to take an interest in soil life, the health of the vines, and the balance in nature. It is quite simply inspiring to see, experience, and taste how top producers all over the world are working nowadays. Not every wine grower or winery has signed up to this approach yet, but the numbers are increasing year by year. For a real wine lover it is essential to understand how great wines are produced, especially in the vineyard.

Left: By their very nature, old vines give low yields of well-balanced grapes.
Top: Cultivating steep slopes is worth the effort. The best wines often come from extreme locations.

The grapevine

The grapevine is a long-lived, perennial plant, and unlike annual plants, it can exist in one spot for a number of years—around 30, on average. Grapes are produced at the end of the grapevine's yearly lifecycle, but the individual stages of development leading up to this point are not independent events: Each successive stage is the result of the preceding one. Buds that develop in year N, for example, were formed in the spring and summer of the previous year (N-1).

If the plant was exposed to diseases or climatic events such as hailstorms during that year, they would affect not only the crop of the N-1 vintage, but that of vintage N as well.

The vine is a woody plant with herbaceous elements. Its perennial structures (the stock, scion, and roots) store starch, carbohydrates, and other supplies. These essential energy reserves enable the plant to survive the winter and guarantee that there will be growth in the spring, producing new leaves to take over the role as energy provider.

The vine draws all the raw materials it needs for growth and grape produc-

The vines start to shoot in late spring. Soon after the first young leaves have appeared, the buds which will produce bunches of grapes also begin to form, growing straight upwards.

tion from the surrounding natural environment in which it was planted. Its root system draws water and minerals from the soil and converts them into various growth hormones that circulate around the plant as required. As soon as temperatures start to rise at the beginning of spring, sap can be seen flowing where the canes have been pruned. Winegrowers speak of the vines "crying" or "bleeding;" this signals the start of the growth cycle.

The part of the vine that grows above ground is woody, and consists of the trunk (stock and scion) and biennial canes. The latter can be long or short, depending on pruning, and their buds sprout the annual shoots, some of which will bear grapes. Photosynthesis takes place in the vine leaves, as with all chlorophyll-containing plants: The chlorophyll absorbs the sunlight, which enables the leaves to extract carbon dioxide (CO_2) from the air and

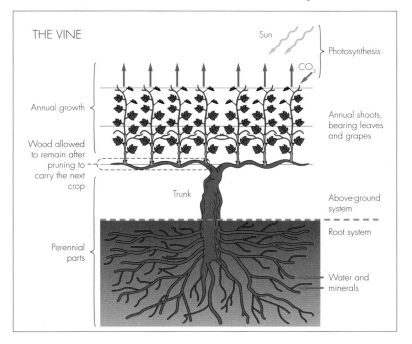

THE VINE

Sun

Photosynthesis

CO_2

Annual growth

Annual shoots, bearing leaves and grapes

Wood allowed to remain after pruning to carry the next crop

Trunk

Above-ground system

Root system

Perennial parts

Water and minerals

During the growth phase, nutrients are primarily sent to the tips of the canes and to the flowerheads. Under optimal conditions, growth stops during the ripening phase, and the carbohydrates are redirected to the berries and the green parts of the plant. They are stored in the grapes as sugar, and in equal measure as glucose and fructose in the green parts, and as starch in the woody part of the vine.

convert it into sugar. The energy obtained in this way is used to produce a variety of fundamentally different substances over the course of the vegetative process. These substances include hundreds of aroma compounds, which are stored in the grapes (see diagram on previous page).

Many factors influence the quality of the grape harvest, and consequently that of the wine as well. The nutrients needed for growth and fruit production are drawn from the air and the soil, which means that both the above-ground and the below-ground parts of the vine must be cultivated in order to achieve the best possible development.

The amount of foliage exposed to the sun, through which photosynthesis occurs, is of central importance. Winegrowers sup-port the process by creating an optimal canopy surface area and thus a balanced leaf to fruit ratio. Vine density, row orientation, and the height of the trellises can all be tailored to help achieve this. If the number of vines per acre is kept low (1,200 to 1,600 per acre or 3,000 to 4,000 per hectare, for example), the rows can be planted further apart, increasing the amount of sunlight that reaches the ground. To balance this out, the height of the canopy can be raised (tall, broad vines) or the tops of the trellises opened up by training each vine into a lyre shape. If the vines are planted more densely (around 3,200 to 4,000 per acre, or 8,000 to 10,000 per hectare), there will be a few casualties, but the canopy can be thicker. In such cases, the vigor of the vines must be controlled by not over-using fertilizer, and, if necessary, by removing summer shoots and side shoots to increase ventilation. In practical terms, therefore, this means that the more densely the vines are planted, the more work is required to tend them, and thus the higher the production costs will be.

The onset of veraison (the period when the grapes start to change color) signals the end of the vine's vegetative growth, when sugar starts to accumulate in the fruit. If ripening does not take place, energy supplies are principally directed toward the tips of the shoots. The end of vegetative growth is a natural process accelerated by lack of water. Hence, heavy rain during this phase can significantly disrupt the ripening process. High atmospheric humidity also brings with it the risk of diseases from molds and fungi.

Nature takes its course in the Lot region: old vines

Vineyard with widely spaced rows in Hawke's Bay, New Zealand

A further factor affecting the quality of the crop is the yield capacity of the vine. Suppose that two almost identical vines, with the same root system and the same leaf surface area exposed to the sun's rays, have equal reserves of energy. If one vine has to share these nutrients among eight bunches of grapes, while the other only has four to supply, the berries of the first vine will have a lesser concentration not only of sugar, but also of color and flavor. Consequently, the grower must find a balance between yield size and quality that will allow the crop to ripen sufficiently, but also provide a viable level of income per acre (hectare).

If the size of the crop in a newly-planted vineyard is too high, the quality of the grapes will be lower; the process of storing reserves of nutrients in the roots and woody part of the vine suffers, and this has long-term negative consequences for the plant.

Varieties of grape

There are hundreds of grape varieties worldwide, although only a few of these have real economic importance. Wine grapes are varieties of the species *Vitis vinifera*, and each has distinguishing characteristics, such as the shape of the leaves and grapes, the presence of tiny hairs, or the color of the young foliage. Different

Certain grape varieties, such as Touriga Nacional in the Douro Valley, are easily identifiable even in the autumn, because their foliage turns such an intense color.

varieties also have varying degrees of susceptibility to diseases and frost.

Wine lovers are primarily interested in the produce of these *vinifera* varieties. The wines differ in appearance, smell, taste, and in the balance of alcohol and acidity.

Some varieties, for example, lose a great deal of their acidity as the fruits become riper and their sugar content increases. If the grower waits too long before harvesting these grapes, the wines tend to be rather heavy. Other varieties, such as Riesling, Mosel, the Petit Manseng of Jurançon wines, and the Chenin Blanc of Coteaux du Layon, have the ability to concentrate the sugar while at the same time retaining a good level of acidity.

Certain grape varieties can be recognized by their distinctive smell, such as the Muscat varieties or Gewürztraminer. Others are given away by their color, like the very dark Tannat or the much lighter Spätburgunder. The latter requires particularly favorable climatic conditions to achieve a color of sufficient intensity during the ripening phase, and thus cannot be grown successfully everywhere. Some grape varieties are much more adaptable to the local conditions, however, such as Chardonnay, which can be found all over the world.

Nevertheless, grape variety alone is not the deciding factor. Depending on the properties of the soil in which the vine is planted, the local climate, yield size, and methods of production, the character of wines made from a particular variety can vary considerably.

The wine grape

The wine grape consists of the flesh, skin, and seeds. With the exception of the colored *teinturiers* planted in some countries, even red grape varieties have white flesh. The phenolics are found in the skins and seeds, as well as in the stalks of the grape (pedicel) and the bunch (peduncle). The aroma compounds are also located mainly in the skins of the berries.

The transfer of these substances into the wine takes place either before or during alcoholic fermentation, depending on the grape variety. In red grapes, it is achieved by fermenting the must in contact with the skins of the berries, whereas with white grapes, this kind of maceration is seldom employed. The size of the berries determines the ratio of juice to solids. Large berries have a lot of juice and little skin, but it is more difficult to extract the color and flavor. The size of the berries is dependent upon the grape variety, but it is also influenced by the vigor of the individual vine and by the availability of water.

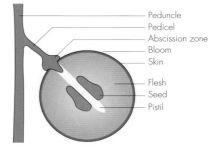

Peduncle
Pedicel
Abscission zone
Bloom
Skin
Flesh
Seed
Pistil

Cross-section through a grape

There can be qualitative differences even with a single grape variety, as a result of the crossings and mutations that can occur naturally within a site. All the vines of a particular clone have been produced from a single original plant, and are therefore identical. Their health is guaranteed in principle, because they are required to be free of disease. Nevertheless, some growers refuse to use clones because they fear that their wines will become standardized.

There is unique potential inherent in every grape.

Premium grape varieties

Chardonnay: Originating in Burgundy (France), where it produces such contrasting wines as the mineral-tasting Chablis and the multi-faceted, mouth-filling Montrachet, Chardonnay has conquered the world. The reason for this is its adaptability in terms of climate, soil, and methods of winemaking. All over the world, the Chardonnay grape produces, at the very least, pleasant wines, and very convincing, great wines if given the appropriate commitment. It is also better suited than any other white grape to vinification and maturation in barrels.

Sauvignon Blanc: Related to the Cabernet varieties, Sauvignon Blanc is often blended with Semillon, where it shows its class in great dessert wines, or the dry Graves Bordeaux. Wines made from Sauvignon Blanc alone first appeared in the Loire (France), in Sancerre and Pouilly-Fumé, which reveal the aromas of blackcurrants and gooseberries, and have a fresh acidity combined with inimitable mineral overtones. If harvested early, Sauvignon Blanc develops grassy, vegetation aromas. It has become the second most popular white variety after Chardonnay.

Riesling: Also known as Rhine Riesling and Johannisberg Riesling, this is, along with Chardonnay, one of the best white wine varieties in the world. Its homeland is the Rheingau (Germany), where as a superior, fairly late-ripening grape, it produces excellent wines with mineral and fruit dimensions, and also the Mosel valley, which is the most important region for this variety. Riesling retains its acidity as it matures, making it the ideal grape for various types of Spätlese and Auslese wines. It loses its raciness, however, if planted in too warm a climate.

Merlot: *This highly productive variety is suitable both for varietal wines and for blending with stronger, more tannic grapes. The best results are achieved in France, in the Bordeaux region, particularly in Saint-Émilion and Pomerol, where some long-lived wines of the highest quality are produced. It is also popular in Switzerland's Ticino, northern Italy, and south-eastern Europe. Merlot is fruity, velvety, and matures faster than Cabernet, but in pure varietal form has only lately attracted international attention. It is currently being planted at a significant rate.*

Cabernet Sauvignon: *As the basis of the famous crus classés of the French Médoc, this variety has risen to become the most popular red wine grape. Good Cabernet wines are dark red, smell of cedar and blackcurrants, have considerable body and a firm structure, and age extremely well. This late-ripening, robust variety flourishes in warmer climates, delivering high-quality wines in California, Australia, South Africa, Chile, and also Italy and Spain.*

Pinot Noir: *Pinot Noir is responsible for the famous red wines of France's Côte d'Or, and plays an important role in the Champagne region. It was introduced to new areas by Cistercian monks, and found a place in Alsace, Germany, Austria, Switzerland, the northeast of Italy, and eastern Europe. Pinot Noir is one of the most challenging red grape varieties for a grower, since it requires a low yield and the utmost care during vinification to produce wines of convincing quality.*

Most important white

Albariño is the finest white wine variety grown in the Spanish region of Galicia, and one of the greatest white varieties in Europe. Characterized by small, densely clustered grapes with hard skins and many seeds, it delivers average-sized yields in humid climates. Albariño produces the best results when planted on slate or granite. Its elegant wines have complex aromas of exotic fruits, pears, and apples, with discreet vegetation notes and a hint of eucalyptus.

Chenin Blanc: This great French variety from Anjou in the Loire has two distinctive characteristics: It has a high natural acidity and is susceptible to botrytis. Depending on vintage, ripeness, and the intentions of the grower, Chenin from the Loire can produce a whole spectrum of different wines, from sparkling, through bone dry, to wines which have extremely concentrated residual sugars and age well. In California and South Africa, Chenin Blanc is a very versatile grape.

Gewürztraminer has grayish-pink grapes that produce wines with a golden gleam and an unmistakable bouquet reminiscent of roses and Muscat. The low yielding but demanding variety is only really convincing if its grapes are harvested when very ripe. For this reason, it tends to appear as an Auslese or Spätlese, often has a high alcohol content, and is frequently oily. The most interesting wines are produced in Alsace, Germany, Switzerland, Austria, and northern Italy.

wine grape varieties 1

The **Malvasia** family of grape varieties, including an early red variety, probably originated in Asia Minor. It was widely planted throughout Ancient Greece, particularly on the islands, where rich, oily dessert wines are still made from it today, as they are in the Lipari Islands off Sicily, and as Malmsey in Madeira. Malvasia also has a significant presence in central Italy, where, by contrast, it is usually made into dry wines.

Müller-Thurgau: Professor Hermann Müller, from Thurgau in Germany, grew this crossing of Riesling and Chasselas (Gutedel) at Geisenheim in 1882. An early-ripening variety that needs damp, deep soils, Müller-Thurgau delivers high yields, but is very susceptible to mildew and other diseases. Its low acidity produces wines that seem soft and round, and have a subtle hint of Muscat that is lost if the grapes become very ripe. Müller-Thurgau is the most widely planted grape variety in Germany, and is also very important in Austria, the Czech Republic, Slavonia, Slovenia, Hungary, and Luxembourg.

Muscat, Moscato or **Muskateller** – behind the names lies one of the oldest and most ramified families of vines. Most renowned is the Muscat Blanc à Petits Grains, whose small, aromatic grapes are the basis for one of the world's most popular sweet sparkling wines, the Italian Asti, previously known as Asti Spumante. Muscats are grown in many countries, however, and famous examples are Samos and Muscat de Frontignan.

Most important white

Pinot Blanc: Also known as Pinot Bianco, Weißburgunder, and Clevner, this grape variety is a distinct member of the Pinot family. A demanding, but fairly robust variety, it needs well-ripened grapes to develop its character, which is to be found in roundness and good body, rather than in the somewhat discreet aroma. Pinot Blanc plays an important role in northern Italy and the Austrian province of Styria, as well as in Slavonia, Slovenia, Hungary, and Romania.

Pinot Gris: Also known as Pinot Grigio, Grauburgunder, and Ruländer, this robust relative of Pinot Noir has grayish-pink tinted grapes, and requires deep soils. In the 14th century, it arrived in the Lake Balaton area of Hungary from France. In Alsace, Austria, and Germany, it produces Spätlese and Auslese wines which are frequently of the highest quality—full of extractions and extremely rich, with delicate spiciness but little acidity. It is currently enjoying its greatest popularity as Pinot Grigio.

Sémillon: This variety has a tendency to become noble rot, and is responsible for the great sweet wines of Bordeaux. The best dry wines are produced in Pessac-Léognan, also in France. Sémillon wines can age very well, developing aromas of honey, candied fruits, and chocolates, while often retaining a fresh, citrus note. Although planted widely throughout the world, Sémillon only develops real and distinctive character in Hunter Valley, Australia.

wine grape varieties 2

Silvaner: Once the most widely planted variety in Germany, Silvaner has now been driven out by Müller-Thurgau in many areas. It is decidedly neutral if not grown on an eminently suitable site, but can produce wines that are pleasantly dry, moderately acidic, and make a strong impression on the palate. Franconia (Franken), in central Germany, is the most significant region for Silvaner, but it also delivers convincing quality in Alsace, if treated carefully in both vineyard and winery.

Trebbiano: The best-known version of this white wine grape is the Italian Trebbiano Toscano, which was previously one of the main ingredients in Chianti. A relatively neutral-tasting variety, its main use is in France (where it is known as Ugni Blanc) in the distilling of Cognac and Armagnac. Trebbiano's greatest asset is that it delivers extremely high yields while retaining a degree of acidity. Its most important varietal expression is the D.O.C. Trebbiano d'Abruzzo, from the Abruzzi region of Italy.

Palomino is the main grape for manzanilla and sherry. It takes well to the hot, dry soils of Andalusia in southern Spain, particularly the albariza soils around Jerez, where it can easily yield 750 to 900 U.S. gallons per acre (70 to 80 hl/ha). Currently, it is also made into dry, neutral white wines, although it lacks the necessary acidity and aromas, which are added by oxidation and the use of flor yeast. Palomino is grown in Australia for producing sherry-style wines.

Vine cultivation: Pruning the vines

The grapevine is a climbing plant that originally grew up trees. Left to its own devices, it tends to grow horizontally, because the first buds to burst are generally the ones at the very end of the cane tips. The vines should therefore always be pruned to counter this tendency for rampant growth, because it weakens the structure of the plant—the vine becomes fragile, difficult to tend, and little suited to bearing high-quality fruit.

Pruning crucially influences both the quantity and the quality of the yield, by determining how many buds are allowed to remain on the vine. Each bud puts forth a shoot, which in turn bears up to three bunches of grapes. The level of productivity depends on the vine variety and on the location of the buds on the stock.

If the crop is large, there may be too many bunches for the vine's ability to photosynthesize. This results in an unfavorable leaf to fruit ratio and a corresponding difficulty in ripening the grapes. In addi-

Guyot pruning leaves a long cane

Vines are pruned in winter

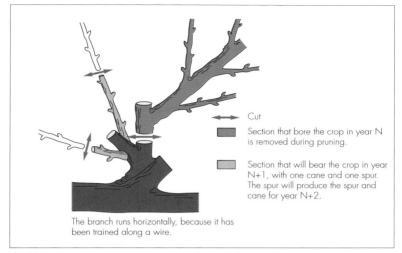

Cut

Section that bore the crop in year N is removed during pruning.

Section that will bear the crop in year N+1, with one cane and one spur. The spur will produce the spur and cane for year N+2.

The branch runs horizontally, because it has been trained along a wire.

Simple Guyot pruning

tion, because the grapes are given priority access to nutrients, the vine itself is weakened as it cannot build up much in the way of reserves. By contrast, if too few buds remain on the vine, the plant does not have sufficient outlet for its growth capabilities. Plant growth may be vigorous (with thick shoots), but the fruit crop will be insignificant. This makes no improvement to the quality of the grapes, but simply leads to a reduction in yield and income. The art of vine pruning lies in finding the ideal compromise for an optimal crop. The general "balance" of the vine must be taken into account, to avoid an overly-dense curtain of foliage. It is also important to limit the number of cuts made to the vine, because these are the entry points for diseases affecting the wood.

The pruning method used will largely depend on the productivity of the particular variety of vine. In productive varieties, every bud will bear bunches of grapes, whereas none will develop from the lower buds of less productive ones. In the former case, "spur pruning" should be used to avoid overproduction; in the latter, only the less severe "cane pruning" method will produce a satisfactory yield. With spur pruning, the canes are cut back to two or three buds. This method is principally employed with vines that are trained into a goblet shape (the gobelet system) or into single or double cordons. Cane pruning involves leaving at least five buds. To prevent the sideways extension of the stock, and in preparation for the following year's pruning, a two-bud spur is also left. This is called Guyot pruning, which can be simple (one spur, one cane) or double (two spurs, two canes). In the double system, the canes are trained unilaterally (on the same side of the stock) or bilaterally (on both sides of the stock) in a bow shape.

The timing of pruning influences the timing of budding. The experienced winegrower will prune as late as possible, and an old German saying holds that "the best pruning is a March pruning" (i.e. in late spring). In some regions of Europe, tradition demands that pruning is not carried out before the feast day of St. Vincent, the patron saint of winegrowers, on January 22. One thing is certain, however: It is vital to wait until all the leaves have fallen and the sap has retreated, because only then will the plant have finished storing up the reserves that will see it through the winter and start growth again in the spring.

The height of the trunk is also deter-

mined by pruning. For mechanical harvesting, it is helpful to increase the height of the trunk. To enable it to grow straight and without cut wounds, the wild shoots growing out from the trunk should preferably be removed during the growth phase. This woody matter can be burned or shredded for compost, which can later be used as mulch for the soil.

Pruning takes a long time, and if the wood is thick, can be difficult and strenuous work. For this reason, attempts have been made to mechanize the process. The advent of pneumatic and electric secateurs was the first step forward, reducing the force needed to cut through the vine. To speed up the operation, some growers now use machines that remove and shred a portion of the vine, much like cutting a hedge. This is 20 to 30 percent faster than hand-pruning.

Simple bow-trained vine

In countries where labor is hard to come by, such as in Australia, attempts are being made to mechanize pruning as fully as possible. One of the most widely-used systems involves pre-pruning the part of the vine that will bear the following year's crop, and completely removing the rest mechanically, so that the wood cannot grow too long. The next year, the roles are reversed. Comparative studies have shown that the crops produced by this method are not as good as those delivered by traditional, manual pruning, due to the uneven distribution of bunches of grapes.

Although pruning partially determines future yield size, it is far from being an exact science. Numerous factors influence the fruitfulness of a particular bud, and the success of flowering and the other stages of the growth phase. If the grape crop is too heavy after flowering, some clusters may be removed. When grapes are pruned before the normal harvest, it is called "green harvesting."

Double bow-trained vine

Most important red

Barbera: Once the stuff of everyday drinking in Piedmont in northern Italy, and now the country's most cultivated grape variety after Sangiovese, Barbera has become a top-quality product in the last two decades. Thanks to the de-acidification process and fermentation in barrels, it now delivers complex, fruity reds with a firm structure and good aging potential. This is true only in Piedmont, however.

Cabernet Franc: It ripens early, making it better suited to cooler regions. The Loire region also produces varietal Cabernet Francs that have an attractive taste of berry fruits, unobtrusive tannins, but often a higher acidity than the mightier Cabernet Sauvignon. Although this variety is often used in light bistro wines, particularly in the northeast of Italy, some first-class, velvety, mouth-filling wines have come out of the Loire in recent years.

Carignan plays an important role as an intensely colored, tannic, blending wine. Although being a highly productive variety, it can be abused. Carignan ripens late and is susceptible to downy and powdery mildew. With low yields and old vines, however, it can deliver extremely characterful wines, such as in Priorat (in Catalonia) or Languedoc (southwestern France), where it is still the dominant grape variety in terms of quantity.

wine grape varieties 1

Dolcetto: Along with Barbera and Nebbiolo, Dolcetto, the "little sweet one," is the third grape variety of Piedmont in northern Italy, and the quickest to ripen. As a result, it was often given the least favorable sites and fermented into wine that was ready to drink early. Dolcetto is now being accorded more attentive treatment. It has an attractive, dark ruby-red color, with wonderful aromas of sweetish berries, quince, and even a delicate hint of almonds.

Gamay owes its fame to Beaujolais. Gamay Noir is planted there at a density of 3,600 to 4,000 vines per acre (9,000 to 10,000 per hectare). The grapes must be picked by hand, because they are usually fermented whole using carbonic maceration. If wines are produced by fermenting the must, however, they have a very interesting potential for aging. Elsewhere, Gamay has gained a permanent foothold only in the Loire and the Ardèche in France, and in Switzerland.

Garnacha Tinta is the most widely planted variety in Spain, where it is produced almost exclusively as young or rosé wines, though it is also combined with other varieties such as Tempranillo. This undemanding variety is not harmed by a hot and arid climate, and contributes body and alcohol to a blend, although it tends to oxidize easily. Only very occasionally does it show its class, such as in the Priorat region of Catalonia, or in France, in Châteauneuf-du-Pape, or the naturally sweet Banyuls wines.

Most important red

Malbec was once widely planted in Bordeaux, but has been superseded there by Merlot. Its main stronghold in France is now Cahors where it is responsible for the region's famous "black wine." Given a medium-sized yield, this dark, tannic variety can deliver characterful reds with good potential for aging. The same is true of Malbec from Argentina, where it is a very popular variety that has produced some interesting, quality wines in recent years.

Monastrell: Also known as Mourvèdre, this is Spain's second most important grape after Garnacha. It usually produces soft, dry, but meaty wines. Although in Spain it is mostly used for reds that are designed to be drunk young, Mourvèdre from the south of France has a different character. Extremely late-ripening and with noble tannins, it plays a role in fine southern Rhône blends, and finds top form in Bandol.

Nebbiolo: Probably the greatest Italian red wine variety, Nebbiolo is grown on little more than 12,500 acres (5,000 hectares) in Piedmont and Valtellina, Lombardy. Barolo, Barbaresco, and a number of other D.O.C. wines owe their multi-layered bouquet (which has notes of tea leaves, roses, spices, and tar), powerful tannin structure, and enormous aging potential to this small-berried variety. Nebbiolo demands the very best sites, or it will not ripen.

wine grape varieties 2

Sangiovese: *The most widely planted red wine variety in Italy is also one of its best. It is the grape responsible for the Tuscan Brunello, Chianti, and Vino Nobile wines, and for the wines of the Torgiano and Montefalco regions in Umbria. In cool years, the late-ripening Sangiovese rarely manages to ripen fully, whereas its wines from warmer vintages are characterized by a lively acidity and delicate tannin structure, and always retain a charming elegance.*

Syrah: *This superb variety from the northern Rhône in France has found success throughout the world. It delivers full-bodied, hefty wines that have excellent tannins and complex aromas, including violets, black cherries, wild herbs, licorice, humus and various spices—a combination that winemakers and consumers are greeting ever more enthusiastically. An early ripener, Syrah has conquered Provence and the whole of the Midi and it is also gaining ground internationally.*

Tempranillo: *Spain's highest-quality vine is also known as Tinta del País, Tinto Fino, Cencibel and Ull de Llebre. Its dark wines typically have an aromatic, fruity character, and their potential for aging in wood is particularly prized. The tannins are soft and sweet. Tempranillo is the main grape variety in La Rioja and Ribera del Duero, and thus responsible for Spain's greatest wines. As Tinta Roriz, it also contributes to some of the best red wines from Portugal.*

Terroir

The same variety of vine planted in different locations can produce wines that differ greatly in terms of both structure and aroma—the "terroir effect." A *terroir* is a defined area in which the physical and chemical conditions of the natural environment, the geographical location, and the climate give rise to specific and identifiable products. Consequently, the term denotes the interaction of a number of factors, including soil, vineyard aspect, climate, vine, and grower.

The nature of the soil depends on a number of factors, not least the geological parent material from which it was created by gradual weathering. The composition of this material (for example, granite, slate, or limestone from the Mesozoic or Tertiary periods) naturally influences the properties of the soil. Physical, chemical and biological processes all play an important role in weathering, although microorganisms are the most industrious agents of soil formation: there are billions of fungi, algae, and bacteria in a patch of live earth, in varying proportions, depending on the conditions. These microflora also affect growth cycles and the interaction between soil and roots. The macrofauna such as worms, snails, mites, and insects are also hard at work, and make a significant contribution to loosening and aerating the soil.

The expression of *terroir* in a vine and its grapes is imparted by live soil that sup-

Chamoson in Valais, Switzerland: granite and gravel

Tavel, south Rhône: pebbles over clay-limestone

plies the plant with the substances it needs for growth and fruit ripening. Nutrients from the minerals in the rock dissolve into the groundwater, and are drawn up by the vines. Of course, mineral or organic fertilizers can be used to supplement the natural supply of nutrients: Nitrogen, phosphorus, potassium, calcium, and magnesium are all important, as are essential micronutrients. However, the expression of *terroir* is lost completely if mineral fertilizers are used too heavily in order to produce a significant increase in yield. For this reason, fertilizers should not be used solely with the vine in mind, as often happens, but primarily with regard for the soil and the microorganisms it contains. This complex task can best be achieved by adding composted organic material, which supplies the soil with the essential elements and nutrients it requires. It will also have

the effect of stimulating the activities of the living organisms in the soil.

Some experts believe that every patch of live soil contains its own specific mix of bacteria and yeasts. They are also to be found on the skins of the grapes and are responsible for fermentation. From this point of view, for optimal expression of the *terroir*, these microorganisms should be allowed to complete the fermentation process by themselves, without the addition of cultured yeasts or bacteria. As a result, more and more wine growers who care about the *terroir* use spontaneous fermentation.

Mosel: steep slope with weathered blueschist

Uffhofen, Rheinhessen: weathered sandstone

Topography and climate

Topography also plays a role in the expression of the *terroir*, in that aspect and water supply influence the lifecycle of the vine—as does climate, in a variety of ways. The wider climatic conditions (for example Mediterranean or continental) determine the climate in the wine region, and thus the length of the active growth phase. The vines used must be suitable for the particular location. In cooler regions, for example, early-ripening vines are preferable. In a low mountain range, factors that must be taken into account include the elevation, aspect, and incline of the plot, and the presence of water courses or forests; sites higher up the slopes tend to be less prone to frost in spring than those lower down or on the valley floor. In regions with a hotter climate, by contrast, where the grapes sometimes suffer from an excess of sugar and a lack of acidity, vineyards at higher elevations produce grapes with a better balance. In the most varied ways, therefore, the interplay of topography and climate influences the character of the grapes and thus of the wine.

In Hessigheim on the River Neckar in Baden-Württemburg, vines are only cultivated on the steep south-facing slopes.

In the Douro valley in northern Portugal, all the slopes on both sides of the river have been terraced and planted.

The combination of conditions in a particular vineyard, such as temperature, exposure to the sun, and humidity, is called the mesoclimate. These all have an effect on the vines, but the parameters can be modified by different methods of vineyard organization and by controlling the vigor of the plants. *Terroir*, then, is a wide-ranging term encompassing all the factors that can influence the typical character of a wine.

Terroirs were historically given fixed boundaries by winemakers who realized that a specific plot of land regularly produced a special wine. Their observations were often made over the course of several generations, and respect for a particular *terroir* became part of a cultural history that the winemaker helped to create. The manner in which a grower cultivates his vineyard gives due regard to soil and choice of grape variety, and handles the grapes in the winery, influences the character of the wine, and can emphasize or obscure the terroir. In the absence of an aware and attentive winemaker, even the best *terroir* will not find convincing expression.

The hilly vineyards in Collioure in the south of France face the Mediterranean, ensuring a degree of humidity.

In Burgundy, monks built walls around the best vineyards during the Middle Ages so that they could be harvested separately.

Soil conditions

The nature of the soil depends on how the geological parent material has been altered and shaped by physical, chemical, and biological processes. In general, soils suitable for viticulture are those that are not particularly fertile or deep. Vines have been, and indeed still are, planted on soils weathered from rocks of various geological periods, from the Paleozoic through to the Quaternary.

The depth of the soil will determine how extensive the spread of the root system will be. A deep soil with extensive water reserves can be used for bulk production. A relatively shallow, dry soil, by contrast, is generally better at delivering greater quality. Soils that are highly compacted or waterlogged, can have a negative effect on root growth.

Soil is made up of a number of constituents, in varying proportions. Silica is the dominant ingredient in the sandy vineyard plots along the coasts of the Mediterranean and in large parts of Australia. In the famous Graves region of Bordeaux, it is present in the form of gravel and fine-grained soils. Loam consists of silica (sand) and clay, and the proportion of each determines the grade. Loamy and clay soils are more compact, and hence less suitable for viticulture. A soil with a high clay content is fairly impermeable. It contracts in dry weather, becoming hard, cracked, and extremely difficult to cultivate. The

Chalk and marl in Chablis

River gravel deposits along the Rhône

organic material in the soil—plant residues, manure, added compost—binds with the clay, and this clay–humus complex is a key factor in stabilizing soils against the dangers of erosion and compaction.

Limestone can also be a component of vine-growing soils, and rootstocks for grafting are selected for their tolerance of lime. Chalky soils tend to be fairly infertile, and produce high-quality wines. Depending on the proportions of the different components (sand, clay, and lime), calcareous soils are described as chalky clay, chalky, or sandy clay soils.

Stony soils are generally good for producing quality wines, but are more difficult to cultivate. The stones help the soil retain water by aiding drainage and preventing direct evaporation. They also store heat during the day and release it at night, which helps the ripening process.

The chemical composition of a soil can include varying amounts of a number of trace and macroelements, such as nitrogen, phosphorus, potassium, calcium, and magnesium, as well as iron, manganese, boron, and several others.

Clay soil in Nackenheim, Germany

Gravel and fine-grained soil at Château Latour

Danger of erosion

The major problems faced by soils are erosion and the washing away of nutrients as water rushes down the slopes during heavy storms. The consolidation of agricultural land can add to the problem: As rows of vines are extended and walls and heaps of stones removed, water can run down the slopes even faster, increasing erosion. The structure of the soil may also be a factor. Soils that are loosely packed but consolidated allow rain to penetrate, whereas if there is a crust on the surface, the water forms rivulets that flow faster and faster and cut deeper and deeper, washing away the topsoil and the nutrients along with it. The earth must then be laboriously transported back up to the vineyard slopes.

One of the factors that aids the stability of the soil is the clay–humus complex. For humus to be created, decomposed organic matter must be added in the form of compost or manure. Most wine-producing countries continue to use mainly mineral fertilizers, however, which do not fulfil this structural purpose. Similarly important are the creatures living in the soil, because they ensure that the soil remains permeable. In between the solid material in soil are pores filled with water or air, ideally constituting 50 percent of the total volume of the soil. If large agricultural machinery is driven across the ground, particularly in damp conditions, the soil is compressed and the pores disap-

Soil under threat

Erosion of exhausted soil

and preventing it

pear; the heavier the equipment, the more the earth is compacted. To maintain the structural stability of the soil, the grower should avoid driving machinery in vineyards during wet weather.

Cultivation of the soil is another means of countering erosion, but must be carried out with care, because on steep slopes it could accelerate the process rather than hinder it.

The problems of erosion can also be countered by growing grass between the rows of vines, in order to stimulate the growth of microorganisms. Here too, however, care is required. Depending on the species chosen, competition with the vines can be so intense that yields are consid-

erably reduced, or the grapes may not get enough nitrogen, which can disrupt alcoholic fermentation. For this reason, such a cover crop is not appropriate in every situation, although it is undoubtedly one of the best ways of looking after the soil. In the end, it is down to the skill of the winemaker to find the best compromise between the desired outcome and the dictates of circumstance.

Counter-measure: durable soil restoration

Counter-measure: ploughed earth

Mechanization

Tractors first appeared in vineyards in the 1950s. Their function, and consequently their appearance, has evolved and changed with time, and from region to region. Small vineyard tractors that drive between rows are used where the vines are sufficiently spaced; they are common in Germany, the south of France, California, and Chile, for example. If the vines are planted closer together, as they are in Burgundy or Champagne, so-called straddle-tractors which span one or two rows are used.

Little by little growers have been forced to adapt their vineyards for mechanization, by planting the vines in rows and as far as possible training the curtain of foliage along wire frames, so that machinery can pass in between. In vineyards that are laid out in terraces, however, such as in Portugal's Douro valley, in Germany along the Mosel and in the Wachau, in France in the north of the Côtes du Rhône, or in any mountainous wine region of the world, it is impossible to mechanize viticulture. Here, the work is done manually, just as it always has been, although heli-

Small power harrows of the type used elsewhere in horticulture can be deployed in densely planted vineyards.

Horses or mules are ideal for tillage in vineyards, because they do not compact the soil.

in the vineyard

In this vineyard the soil is broken up with a cultivator which is operated and drawn by a comparatively lightweight tractor.

In densely planted vineyards, straddle-tractors can negotiate the narrow rows to carry out tasks such as spraying and canopy pruning.

copters are used in some areas for spraying the vines.

The difficulty of mechanizing production is often one of the reasons used to justify elevated prices in industrialized nations, where it is more cost effective, once wages and employer's social security contributions are taken into account, for the work to be done mechanically rather than by hand. Elsewhere in the world—in South America, for example—labor is still very cheap, and wine producers are largely turning back to human workers. Although many tasks are done by specialized machines nowadays, including pest control, soil cultivation, foliage trimming, and to a certain extent, grape picking, one task that has proved difficult to mechanize is the pruning of the vines.

Caterpillars are better at spreading the pressure on the soil.

Cultivation

The primary goal of a winegrower is to produce quality grapes in sufficient quantities to ensure that his business remains viable. Various methods of cultivation can be employed to achieve this, from the traditional, through the judicious use of integrated or organic practices, to biodynamic cultivation. The fundamental differences between them are mainly concerned with the control of pests and diseases in the vineyard, but also with the cultivation of the soil, weed control, use of fertilizers, and finally, the winemaking process itself.

OVER-EXPLOITATION OF VINES AND SOIL

In the period from 1960 to 1980, agriculture as a whole made heavy use of newly available chemicals for controlling pests and diseases. In viticulture, the products were applied at a precisely stipulated stage of vine development, and then, depending on the length of time they remained effective, reapplied at regular intervals. The use of fertilizers was similarly indiscriminate, and could disrupt the natural balance of the soil or lead to an excess of a particular substance such as potassium or nitrates. At the time, people were probably unable—and unwilling—to appreciate the effects that some of these products would have on the environment and consumers, and alternative products and methods of monitoring did not yet exist. Consumers were also slow to tackle such issues, although

Above: Backpack sprayers are still frequently used in small wine-growing estates.

methods

Below: Quality-conscious winemakers use natural rather than artificial fertilizers.

there was a clear interest in alternative and ecological lifestyles as early as the 1970s.

Belief in the miracle of chemistry can be explained by the traumas experienced by winegrowers from the mid-19th century onward, in the form of Oidium (powdery mildew), phylloxera, Peronospora (downy mildew) and black rot. Added to which were World Wars and a global economic crisis. When things began to pick up again in the 1960s, winegrowers and farmers relied on the panaceas of the chemical industry. No-one gave very much thought to the consequences. As a result, vineyards were often over-fertilized, the vines became weakened, and the wines lacked originality. But worst of all, the groundwater became contaminated with nitrates.

Then there was the fixed seasonal routine: the use of herbicides, leading to erosion and the killing off of soil life; insecticides which also destroyed useful creatures and weakened the natural balance; and pesticides that proved harmful to humans, the soil and the environment. Yet these are the methods still used by the vast majority of winegrowers all over the world to protect vines, as a way of guaranteeing sufficient yields from them. As a result, conventional viticulture contributes significantly to environmental pollution in wine-producing countries.

INTEGRATED PRODUCTION

Since the beginning of the 1990s, more and more winegrowers have been switching to what is known as the "integrated" method of cultivation, in which chemical products for pest and disease control are used in a more considered manner. Treatment is only undertaken once the severity of a disease or infestation has reached a certain level. The grower chooses the products that are least harmful to the environment and vineyard worker, and does not deploy them until circumstances are favorable, in order to achieve the best results. The right moment may be determined by the lifecycle of the pest, the stage of development reached by the vine, or by the weather.

Conscientious monitoring in the vineyard is essential if environmentally-friendly agriculture is to be successful and help reduce the use of chemical treatments. However, collecting the necessary information does take time.

What motivates winegrowers to switch to integrated cultivation is not economics, but rather the need to optimize work on the vineyard. Integrated production involves following certain principles regarding fer-

Ploughed vineyard

Grassy intermediate rows

tilizers and soil cultivation. The guidelines recommend growers limit the addition of nitrogen, and shred and compost the matter cut from the vines during pruning, returning it to the soil.

Naturally, all the principles of integrated production are also heeded with organic cultivation. At one end of the scale are growers' own individual practices, very few of which are regulated by any kind of association, and at the other is a set of clearly defined regulations and a system of regular checks. Just a few years ago, organic wines were likely to be squarely in the firing line as far as many wine critics were concerned, but now the position is very different.

In many countries around the world, winegrowers are increasingly prepared to accept the sometimes very lengthy transition period to organic production and the strict rules governing production.

Weather station with sensors

A vineyard's rain gauge

ORGANIC WINEGROWING

Like organic farming in general, organic viticulture does not use chemical and synthetic fertilizers, weed killers, insecticides, fungicides, and acardicides. In the case of winegrowing, however, a much broader approach is needed—preserving the soil and purity of the groundwater, protecting different species and conserving the countryside, and managing the supply and disposal of the entire operation in an ecologically-friendly way.

The life of the soil in the vineyard is fundamental to the whole process. To energize, support and nourish it, winegrowers use organic materials, with compost as the key player.

Planting green cover is especially important in organic viticulture, substituting for crop rotation in general organic farming. This produces thick root penetration in the soil which has a long-term, positive influence on the rich supply of microorganisms. The associated eclectic mixtures of leguminous plants, clovers, grains, grasses, and herbs, which are all mowed and mulched twice or three times, make excellent fertilizers and ensure the formation of humus. The flowers attract insects back into the vineyards, which keeps down the populations of red spider mite and grape vine moth. Planting green cover prevents vineyard erosion and also helps to adjust the water balance.

European viticulture faces the constant threat of powdery mildew (Oidium) and downy mildew (Peronospora). While conventional production relies completely on chemical agents, organic winegrowers are primarily concerned about reducing the risk of infection. To this end they examine and take account of these points:

Manual labor is often essential.

Sowing for green manure in the vineyard

Compost and straw applied in the vineyard

- suitable location
- appropriate grape varieties
- correct space between rows and lines
- the best cultivation system
- limited number of shoots which can be left when first cutting in winter
- pinching off in spring to reduce the shoots per cane to an optimal number
- diligent leaf work which ensures good ventilation during the growing season
- thinning out the grapes if necessary

In conventional viticulture, all of these steps are not taken as a rule: The only exception tends to be estates which are geared to producing top quality and which are already using some organic methods. It is essential for organic winegrowers to avoid problematic locations, or particularly susceptible grape varieties. To strengthen the efficiency of the vines, plant-based infusions and products can be used in addition to stone meals, and the like.

Organic winegrowers have to work in a far more careful and informed way than their conventional colleagues. The successes are reflected in fewer fluctuations in yields and quality, and often in higher must weights as well, even in less favorable years.

As far as the quality of the wine is concerned, winegrowers all agree that it is produced in the vineyard, and that is why organic viticulture is seen as the way ahead.

Dynamizing the horn manure

Horn silica stimulates photosynthesis

BIODYNAMIC CULTIVATION

The theory behind this system holds that disease in a plant (or any other living organism) is an indication that the natural equilibrium has been disturbed. The disease must, of course, be treated, but the main goal is to restore the balance between the plant and its environment. Naturally, this cannot be achieved overnight, just as growers cannot switch from their previous practices to biodynamic methods in the space of a day.

Biodynamic agriculture originated in Germany at the beginning of the 20th century, under the influence of the anthroposophist Rudolf Steiner. His concept, which is also the basis of a philosophy and system of education, can be applied to all branches of agriculture. Steiner saw the relationship between nature and the cosmos as a holistic system in which everything is interconnected, working in mutual cooperation. While he attempted to harness these influences, he also recommended the use of specific preparations, in the case of viticulture to strengthen the vines and boost their immunity.

The two main preparations of biodynamism are horn dung and horn silica. In much the same way as homeopathy, it is not a matter of administering material doses, but of providing stimulation. For the "horn dung 500" preparation, a cow's horn is filled with the animal's manure and buried in the soil in fall. According to Steiner's theory, the cosmic forces in the earth are stored during the winter and enrich the dung. In spring, it is dynamized by stirring it vigorously in large amounts of water, and it is then applied to the vineyard soil. Horn dung strengthens the soil and plays the major role in its revitalization.

Horn silica, preparation 501, is made by filling a cow's horn with finely ground silica and burying it in spring. It is dug out again in fall, likewise dynamized with water and applied to the soil. It stimulates the vines and improves the photosynthesis process, which is a significant factor in less sunny cultivation regions. Compost enriched with plant-based preparations is equally important.

The cosmic influence on the vines varies with the position of the nine planets of the solar system, the twelve constellations, the sun, and the moon. The effects of the various procedures intensify if this influence is respected. The sowing calendar, which is published every year, gives detailed advice for each day.

Biodynamic grower Jacob Duijn

The biodynamic viewpoint holds the use of agrochemicals responsible for a series of problems. Herbicides destroy the living organisms in the soil and hinder healthy vine growth. Plants whose balance is thus disrupted attract parasites and diseases, but the agents used to treat the condition cause further disturbances in the soil. This eliminates the influence of the *terroir*, and the wines lose their typical character.

The biodynamic route is not an easy one, as there are no universally applicable remedies. Very wet or extremely dry conditions require different approaches. Each biodynamic winegrower must find the best individual solution for his or her vineyards.

Ladybugs, nature's pest controllers

Integrated vine protection

The aim of pest management is of course to ensure all-round healthy vines and the production of healthy grapes for wine making or directly for the table for consumption as dessert grapes.

Integrated pest management concerns not only direct means of control, but also a large number of indirect measures. The integrated concept involves maintaining vine diseases and infestations below the threshold where they would become economically damaging, using all the financially, ecologically, and toxicologically justifiable methods of damage control available.

Methods of Damage Control

VITICULTURAL METHODS
The aim of these methods is to increase the vine's natural resistance on the one hand, and at the same time to engineer the vineyard mesoclimate in such a way that disease pathogens and vine pests do not find the living conditions they need. This includes the choice of a vine variety suitable for the location, appropriate use of fertilizer, and timely pruning to ensure good ventilation.

PHYSICAL AND MECHANICAL METHODS

In addition to mechanical weed control, this category principally includes acoustic and visual methods of scaring off birds, the use of bird nets to protect the ripening grapes, and plastic mesh sleeves to prevent damage caused by wild animals trying to eat the plants.

BIOLOGICAL METHODS

Biological pest control involves countering harmful organisms using other organisms. Integrated pest management in viticulture currently allows the use of two such agents: first, preparations of *Bacillus thuringiensis*, which are used to control grape berry moths, and second, the fungal pathogen *Metarhizium anisopliae*, which is harmful to the black vine weevil. Natural pest control can also be significantly aided if the grower treats vines with chemicals that do not harm beneficial insects. This is particularly true in the case of the predatory mite *Typhlodromus pyri*, which can remain unaffected if an appropriate agent is chosen, so that direct intervention to control the spider mite is seldom necessary.

BIOTECHNOLOGICAL METHODS

The natural reactions of pests to chemical or physical stimuli are exploited as a means of combating them. Yellow, white or red colored disks may be used, for example, as scarers, as with the cultivation of fruit crops and ornamental plants. Currently, the method with the greatest practical significance in this category is the use of

Vineyard scent dispensers continuously release sexually enticing pheromones which disorient the male grape berry moth, thereby preventing impregnation of the female. This is known as the confusion method.

Moths on a sticky insect trap

This method also makes use of synthetically produced pheromones of the female grape berry moths. The male moths can detect even the tiniest concentrations of these chemicals via their antennae, and when they do, they follow the trail to the source of the pheromones. Under natural circumstances, they would find the female who is secreting the scent.

In the confusion method, the synthetic pheromones are contained in plastic dispensers, which are evenly distributed throughout the vineyard at a density of around 200 per acre (500 per hectare). The pheromones continuously diffuse from these dispensers into the surrounding environment, flooding the treated area. The male moths become disoriented and confused, because they can no longer detect a trail of pheromones. Finding a partner is no longer possible. As a result, the females are not impregnated, and can only lay unfertilized eggs. This method can be used to control both types of grape berry moth—cochylis (*Eupoecilia ambiguella*) and eudemis (*Lobesia botrana*). The dispensers need only be deployed once, before the first generation of moths takes flight. The distinguishing feature of the confusion method is that it has a specific effect, targeting only the cochylis and the eudemis moth. Consequently, it does not harm beneficial insects such as predatory mites, ichneumon wasps, lacewings, assassin bugs, and ladybugs. These are the most environmentally-friendly pest control measures currently available.

pheromones (sexual scents). In viticulture, this mainly involves the pheromones of the grape berry moths. "Pheromone traps" can be used as a reliable way of indicating when the pest reaches its flight stage, and thus when there is greatest risk of infestation. The male moths are lured into the traps by scents which mimic the pheromones secreted by female moths, and are caught on the sticky surface at the bottom. By regularly checking the traps the winegrower can determine accurately the peaks of the flight stage and hence the optimal time to treat the vines and avoid unnecessary spraying.

As well as their use for prognostic purposes, pheromones are also employed in combating grape berry moths directly by what is known as the confusion method.

CHEMICAL METHODS

Integrated pest management will always involve chemical agents. It is important that growers aim to use insecticides, acaricides, fungicides, and herbicides only when the pests or disease pathogens exceed the damage threshold. Appropriate thresholds have been worked out for the main pests. In the case of fungal pathogens, preventive measures are often necessary. Nevertheless, improving existing prognostic methods, and developing new ones, has a significant part to play in avoiding unnecessary prophylaxis.

Integrated pest management takes the concerns of environmental protection very much into consideration. Whilst all available means of pest control may be used, winegrowers should give preference to biological and biotechnological methods wherever possible.

Hartwig Holst

Insect trap using sugar water

Vine diseases and pests

Viruses, bacteria, phytoplasma, fungi, mites, insects, and nematodes—the vine has many enemies. Fortunately, they are rarely found in the same place simultaneously. Some diseases and pests are more common in some wine regions than others. Of the 40 or so known vine viruses, those involved in the complex of diseases known as fanleaf degeneration occur most frequently. These viruses are spread by threadworms (nematodes), and infected vines may suffer extremely reduced yields. Fanleaf degeneration is combated by only planting healthy vines (following strategies similar to those used in tree nurseries), and by allowing cleared vineyards to lie fallow for a period before they are replanted. Care must be taken to remove as much root material as possible, so that the nematodes have nothing to live on and die of starvation. Treating the soil with agents to kill nematodes is

Powdery mildew: Individual berries have split open.

Phomopsis infection: pycnidia (the spore receptacles) on winter wood

harmful to the environment, and so the practice is banned in some countries (Germany and Switzerland, for example), whilst other countries (such as France) impose tight controls.

Two significant vine diseases are caused by phytoplasma, organisms similar to bacteria: Pierce's disease, which causes a great deal of damage in the U.S.A.; and *flavescence dorée*, which mainly occurs in the south of France.

Certain harmful fungi attack the trunk of the vine and can cause it to die, while others damage the green parts of the vine (leaves, shoots, and grapes). The first group includes the diseases eutypa dieback and esca. To limit their spread the grower must prune the vines without creating large wounds through which the fungi can enter. It is essential that dead rootstocks are burned, otherwise they can become new sources of infection. Of the second group of fungi, three are particularly widespread: downy mildew (*Plasmopara*), powdery mildew (*Oidium*), and gray rot (*Botrytis*).

Downy mildew primarily attacks the leaves, and to such an extent that the vine sheds them before time. This severely affects photosynthesis, reduces the concentration of fructose in the grapes, and alters the composition of the nutrient reserves in the roots of the vine. Copper is an important active ingredient for controlling downy mildew. Commonly used preparations are copper oxychloride and

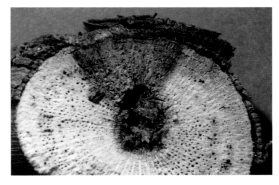

Eutypa dieback: cross-section through a trunk

Esca disease

Bordeaux mixture (copper neutralized with lime).

Organic substances used to control fungal diseases can be divided into three categories: products that work on the contact principle, and thus only protect the organs to which they are applied (contact fungicides); products that penetrate the treated organs and stop the attack within the plant (locally systemic fungicides); and products that penetrate and spread throughout the vine (systemic fungicides).

Powdery mildew can colonize foliage and grapes, causing a reduction in quality or even the loss of the crop. Not all vine varieties are equally susceptible: Some, such as Carignan, are very prone to infection; others, such as Syrah or Pinot Noir, less so. Once the fungus has taken hold, however, it is very difficult to treat, and so preventative measures are essential. Oidium control is generally undertaken using preparations containing sulfur. Organically-based products are also available, and should be deployed only once or twice a year, to prevent the appearance of resistant strains of fungus.

The third great enemy of the vine is *Botrytis*, or gray rot, which can affect both the quantity and the quality of the yield. It is best combated through the use of preventative strategies that promote the vitality of the vine and ensure good ventilation in the canopy. This necessitates reducing the amount of nitrogen added to the soil, training the vines

Grape berry moth 1

Grape berry moth 2

so that they have adequate space, and undertaking work on the canopy (removing the secondary shoots; thinning out the foliage) in good time.

The two types of grape berry moth, cochylis (*Eupoecilia ambiguella*) and eudemis (*Lobesia botrana*), are significant vine pests. They produce two or three generations every summer, and their various larval stages damage the buds, the immature flowers, and the maturing grapes.

The chosen methods of control must be appropriate for the particular stage of development (eggs or larvae), and be deployed at the right time. The less harmful the products are to the environment, vineyard-workers, and beneficial insects, the more precisely an optimal treatment date must be determined; in some cases, one or two days can make a great deal of difference. There are, however, other options available as well.

Willow beauty caterpillar

Black vine weevil

Grapevine phylloxera

The phylloxera louse arrived in France around 1860, in vines imported from the United States. The tiny, yellow insect appeared in England for the first time in 1863, and in the same year, growers in the southern Rhône area of France noticed a vine disease that they had never seen before. The French scientist, Jules Planchon, originally named the pest that was responsible *Phylloxera*, but nowadays it is known scientifically as *Daktulosphaira vitifoliae*. By the end of the 19th century, phylloxera had spread to almost all the wine-producing countries of Europe. Today, it is present in almost all the wine regions of the world.

Phylloxera damages vines primarily by attacking the roots. This causes sustained disruption of the plant's food supply, and even the death of the vine. There is still no really effective chemical treatment. One measure that was used successfully in the past, and is still valid today, is grafting. The scions of susceptible vine varieties (of the species *Vitis vinifera*) are grafted onto phylloxera-resistant rootstocks (hybrids of *Vitis berlandieri*, *Vitis riparia*, and *Vitis rupestris*).

The phylloxera louse finds a new host not by moving to a new plant, but by moving from the leaves to the roots of the vine. The winter eggs laid by the sexual form of the insects hatch at the beginning of the vine's vegetative phase. Once they are fully developed, the young fundatrix lice (stem mothers) create leaf galls, in which they lay their eggs. The "crawlers" that hatch from these eggs spread out over the shoots and create new galls on the young foliage. In late summer, the crawlers no longer head toward the tips of the shoots, but move down the vine and seek out its roots—beginning the underground phase of the cycle. The crawlers migrate first to the deeper layers of the soil, where they spend the winter. The following spring, they feed on young roots, causing swellings and growths, and complete their development as egg-laying females. Parthenogenesis produces several generations of root-living crawlers. Some of the crawlers become nymphs (lice with

| Dotted with leaf galls | Leaves stunted by galls | Eggs and young lice in the gall |

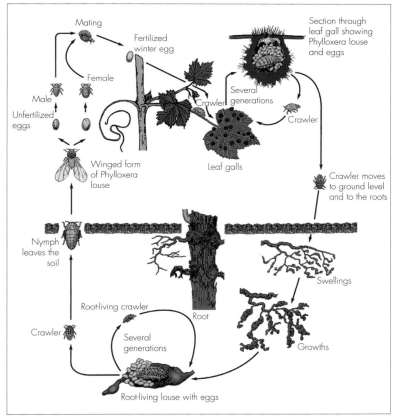

Development cycle of the Phylloxera louse

wing buds) and leave the soil, beginning the above-ground phase of the cycle. The nymphs become winged adults, and seek out American vines on which they lay both large and small eggs. The large eggs hatch into females, while the small eggs produce males. After mating, the female lays only one egg—called a winter egg—on the trunk of the vine. During the next vegetative phase, a new fundatrix louse will hatch from the egg, and the cycle begins again.

Hartwig Holst

Viticulture throughout the year

Grapevines demand constant and careful attention. The work carried out on both the soil and the plants is crucial for the quality of that season's wine, but also lays the foundations for the following year. The techniques used to cultivate the soil depend on the grower's chosen methodology. Chemical weedkilling employs herbicides that reduce the need for manual or mechanical soil cultivation. However, the soil is generally cultivated once or twice a year to loosen and aerate it. This can be done in the fall, or in spring, or in both seasons.

Another possibility is to target the use of herbicides only along the rows of vines. Following this, the ground in between the rows is either cultivated or planted with a grass cover crop. The most promising course of action combines various methods of cultivation: piling up earth around the trunks of the vines and tilling, leveling, or hoeing the soil in between, as necessary. The layer of earth around the graft zone serves to protect the vine from the effects of very cold spells in winter. The piles of earth must be removed in the spring to

Newly planted vine

Grafted rootstock

Ploughing a Mosel vineyard

prevent the scion from growing under the soil and putting down unwanted roots.

The frequency of weeding will depend on the extent of the weed population. Following rain, it can sometimes be difficult to drive tractors across the plots. If the grass is to be a permanent feature, it will have to be mown several times per season. To reduce competition during the growth period, however, some growers prefer temporary coverage: the grass is destroyed at the end of the winter, either by mechanical soil cultivation or with herbicides.

Once again, however, there is no solution that can be applied in all situations. The soil's properties, access to the plot, the problems of erosion, spring frosts, competition for water, and operating costs all have to be taken into account.

There is also a series of tasks to be undertaken to look after the vine. The best time to repair trellises, stakes, and wires is during the winter, usually after pruning. If the cane pruning method has been used, the cane is fastened to the wire of the trellis. As soon as growth has begun, superfluous shoots are removed to aid ventilation in the canopy and make pruning easier the following winter. The water shoots (i.e. shoots growing directly from the trunk) should also be removed, either at the same time or later on. If the vineyard uses a cordon training system, the shoots must be tied up with trellis wire as soon as they are long enough, and fastened along the wires between the stakes. This work has to be done manually, and the canopy should be trimmed at the same time.

The leaves of the vines grow so thickly, especially in the damper wine-growing regions, that they have to be pruned to let light and air get to the vine stocks.

In cooler regions, growers may decide to remove a certain number of bunches per vine around midsummer (i.e. just before veraison), to ensure a high-quality crop. This practice is mainly used with red grape varieties to increase the concentration of color compounds, and is known as "crop thinning" or *vendange verte*.

Spring is also the time to put in new stakes.

In spectacular hillside positions such as these along the Mosel, the winegrowers use ropes to move ploughs and other equipment. The best sites cannot be maintained without using such aids.

When grapes ripen

Between budbreak at the end of the winter and ripe grapes at the beginning of fall, the vine goes through a number of stages of development, some of which are particularly important. At the beginning of the process, the buds get thicker, and gradually the first leaves start to appear. By the time the first five or six have properly unfolded, the bunches of grapes can already be identified. The success of fruit set is governed by the weather and health of the plant during the previous year, and gives an indication of likely yield-size. These small, upright grape clusters and their supporting shoots then continue to develop.

In the northern hemisphere, flowering occurs between the middle of May and the middle of June, depending on the region. Although every flower bud blossoms, not

A leaf bud grows from a node.

The bud opens.

Fully-opened bud

all will produce a grape, because some will drop off either before or after pollination. Young berries can also drop off in the two weeks after flowering.

At fruit set, the bunches of grapes tend to grow horizontally. Once the berries become pea-sized, the bunches sag and hang downwards.

During the stage known as veraison, the grapes of white varieties gradually become translucent, and red varieties begin to develop their color. The shoots now stop growing and metabolic function is directed entirely toward the grapes. The process of ripening begins and sugar accumulates in the berries as they are given priority access to the products of photosynthesis. At the same time, levels of acidity drop. Although the amount of tartaric acid in the grapes remains relatively constant, it increases as a proportion of the overall acid content, due to the sharp fall in the level of malic acid.

Physiological ripeness is reached when the grapes achieve sufficiently high sugar levels without losing too much acidity. In cooler regions, it can sometimes be difficult to achieve the minimum sugar content

Bunches of grapes will form from these flower buds.

Flowering, or inflorescence

A cluster forming

prescribed by the appellation. In hotter regions, by contrast, the problem is more likely to be too great a loss of acidity. In both cases, corrections can be made during the winemaking process.

In addition to physiological ripeness, the ripeness of the aromatic and phenolic compounds must be taken into account. Aromatic ripeness is the point at which the grapes are richest in aromas or aroma-forming compounds. To assess phenolic ripeness, the grower must monitor the development of anthocyanins and tannins, the former being responsible for the color,

the latter guaranteeing the structure of the wine, and, in the long term, the stability of the color. As the grapes ripen, the concentration of anthocyanins increases until a peak is reached, after which the level drops again. Harvesting should ideally take place when this maximum is achieved, but analyzing the concentrations is expensive and tricky, and thus rarely carried out. If the grape variety is suitable for the *terroir*, aromatic and phenolic maturity will usually be achieved as soon as the grapes are physiologically ripe.

In some wine-producing regions, the

A young grape cluster in July

The grapes grow for 100 days.

Pinot Noir grapes starting to change color

date when harvesting may begin is officially controlled, and special permission must be obtained if an earlier harvest seems advisable. The date is determined by the trade associations on the basis of tests carried out in the vineyards. There is no such regulation in the New World and even in Europe things are starting to become more flexible. In Germany, for instance, the rules have been relaxed in recent years to allow producers greater creative freedom. The object of the harvesting ban is to prevent growers picking the grapes too early—fearing bad weather,

for example. They are free to harvest as late as they wish, however. Harvesting is organized on each estate sector by sector, according to which grape varieties ripen first. In some regions, as much as four to six weeks may pass between bringing in early-ripening white varieties and late-ripening red varieties, to say nothing of late-picked grapes for Trockenbeerenauslesen or Eiswein, which cannot be done before a heavy frost.

Ripe Riesling grapes

Pinot Noir grapes during veraison

Overripe grapes with noble rot

Manual harvesting

Growers may opt to harvest their crop manually, or be forced to do so on account of the local conditions. If the slopes are steep, the plots small and fragmented, or the vines old and low, there is often no other choice that is available. Elsewhere, harvesting machines can be used, but many winemakers still decide to pick the grapes by hand.

One of the most important reasons for choosing manual harvesting is to deliver the grapes to the winery in perfect condition. It is advisable to transport the grapes in crates, so that if they are damaged, the juice can run away before it oxi-

dizes. If the crop is in good health, and arrives in the winery as unscathed as possible, the need to add sulfur can be significantly reduced, or even avoided completely. Grapes that are crushed and have spent several hours in the sun are plainly less interesting from the point of view of quality.

Reliable grape pickers will also carefully remove unripe or damaged grapes.

A bunch of Pinot Noir grapes being carefully cut off a young shoot.

Manual harvesting allows the grapes to be sorted during and directly after picking, before they have even left the vineyard. In addition, this method gives the winemaker the option of only destemming a proportion of the yield. Mechanical harvesting does not allow such a choice, because the machine removes only the grapes from the vines, and not their stalks.

Economic factors are not such a crucial consideration for the top châteaux and estates, and they may decide to retain hand-picking for the sake of tradition, even though it is a costly procedure. Where small harvesting teams of not more than 10 or 20 people are used, the atmosphere during the harvest is usually very convivial, with the same pickers often returning year after year

because they enjoy working together. Many growers are unwilling to sacrifice this aspect of the process, and stress that they consider it one of the high points of the viticultural year.

Grape picking on a steep slope with a heavy iron bin

Harvesting is a strenuous business, and carrying and emptying the baskets puts a terrible strain on the body.

Mechanical

Harvesting machines are used for economic and technical reasons. In France, for example, mechanical harvesting costs on average two to three times less than hand picking, once wages and employers' social security contributions are taken into account. Of course, the same is not true in countries where wages and contributions are lower. In some New World countries, for instance Australia, the lack of vineyard labor makes mechanical harvesting essential.

One of the advantages of mechanical harvesting is that it can be used as circumstances dictate. Harvesting can be done at night, while it is cool, and work can continue around the clock if the crop must be brought in urgently, perhaps because the grapes are very ripe or the weather is bad. Confirmed users of mechanical harvesting also express satisfaction at no longer having to worry about providing facilities, food, and accommodation for the pickers.

These benefits are of no use, however, if quality suffers as a result. Not all grape varieties are equal in this respect: Mechanical harvesting works very well with Chardonnay, for example, but less well with Pinot Noir, if it is intended for wines with aging potential.

Top: Mechanical harvester in action
Center: The speed of the machine and the quality of the harvested grapes are closely linked.
Bottom: Grapes are transferred to another vehicle moving in tandem with the harvester.

Harvesting

The quality of the work done by a mechanical harvester also depends on the shake setting and the speed with which it moves. The quicker it passes along the rows, the harder it has to shake the vines to loosen the grapes. This damages the crop, injures the vines, and breaks the stakes. If good quality is to be achieved using mechanical harvesting, a few changes also have to be made in the winery. With white grape varieties, which are particularly susceptible to oxidation, the time between picking and pressing must be kept as short as possible. In some cases, this can mean acquiring an additional grape press.

Mechanical harvesters cannot be used where wines are made by pressing whole bunches (such as Champagne, Crémant, Beaujolais, and Sauternes wines in France), because the machines deliver only individual grapes. This is why the rules governing some appellations expressly forbid the use of mechanical harvesters and require the grapes to be picked by hand.

Top: Intact grapes
Center: Whether undamaged or not, the journey to the winery should not be too long.
Bottom: A mechanical harvester even takes over the laborious task of destemming the grapes.

In the winery

Anyone entering a winery, whether it's a small producer, a large estate, or a cooperative, will usually be surprised at how clean it is. Hygiene has become part of wineries all over the world with the advent of enology: The first diploma in the science of wine was set up in Montpellier in 1955. Every winemaker wants, after all, to convert grape must into wine without any problems and to ensure there are no unwanted bacterial effects on the work of the yeast. As stainless steel is easy to clean and therefore very hygienic, gleaming steel tanks often squeezed out old barrels, vats, and concrete tanks.

Another measure followed hot on the heels of knowledge about temperature's influence on fermentation—temperature control became the gold standard in wineries. This process was accelerated after the extremely hot summer of 1982, which caused major problems in many wineries. Not only can fermentation processes be controlled as required, it can also prevent "stuck fermentation" (when the yeast action becomes dormant unintentionally). This allows aromas to be retained at a level of intensity that had seldom been achieved before. Other methods and technologies have been added to the repertoire. Today's wine lovers can choose from a wide selection of quaffable wines due to the development of modern cellar technology.

However, wine would not hold such fascination if it were a product that could just be controlled by technical means. The extent to which individual winemakers use technology is down to their own personal ambition and philosophy. Just as wine growers swear by natural working practices in the vineyard, they usually want to interfere as little as possible in the winery's natural processes as well. In extreme cases they tip the grapes into amphoras, almost the way it was done when viticulture began; the containers are then sealed, and after a few months they are surprised by the result. To fully appreciate and understand wine, it helps immensely to take a look at the winery.

Left: An example of a red wine fermentation room with high-quality oak vats
Above: Pumping over is a common technique to keep the cap submerged.

Delivery of the harvest

The first step after harvesting is to sort the grapes. This is carried out on special tables, either in the vineyard or as soon as the grapes arrive in the winery. Leaves and any grapes that are unripe or affected with gray rot are removed. Sorting is particularly important for red wine production to avoid negative consequences during maceration and fermentation, but can only be done effectively if the grapes are intact, i.e. have been damaged as little as possible in the course of transportation.

Manual sorting can be dispensed with if the grapes have been harvested mechanically. A

correctly set harvesting machine will not pick shrivelled up or unripe grapes, and rotten ones drop off at the slightest touch of the vine. Leaves are largely removed by fans on the machine.

The crop will arrive in the winery either loaded directly onto a trailer, or in vats,

In large wineries making mass-produced wines, the grapes are delivered in large trailers.

A tipping mechanism empties the crop from the trailer.

baskets, or crates. Where possible, shallow containers that can hold only a small amount should be used, to prevent the grapes from being crushed under their own weight and releasing juice which will oxidize. The longer the journey between vineyard and winery, and the higher the temperature of the air, the more important this factor becomes. Ideally, crates should be emptied by hand; this allows the grapes to arrive in the winery almost unscathed. Small vats should be emptied with forks or derricks. Some vehicles have beds that tip; others have a continuous screw (Archimedes screw) in the floor that conveys the crop to the winery via a large hose. A self-emptying container with a slowly revolving screw of large diameter can give satisfactory results if not overfilled. Next, the grapes are crushed and/ or destemmed (separated from the stalks of the bunch). These operational measures can vary considerably, depending on the grape variety, the pressing and fermentation, and hence the wine style the producer is aiming for.

High-quality grapes are brought to the winery in small crates and emptied by hand.

The undamaged bunches are tipped into a destemmer.

The crop is transported to the winery in small crates.

At the winery, the crates are loaded onto a conveyor belt one by one.

At the end of the conveyor belt the boxes are emptied automatically onto the sorting table.

The workers check the health of the grapes.

are selected

Unripe or unhealthy grapes are removed by hand.

From the sorting table, the bunches are fed into a destemmer.

The stalks and bunchstems leave the winery on a conveyor belt.

Outside, they drop into a trailer to be taken away.

Fine wine and mass-produced wines

To make a good wine, you need good grapes. This ought to be the principle guiding every winemaker. From a practical point of view, it is much easier to make wine using healthy, ripe grapes than ones that are damaged and not ripe enough. Consequently, wine production really begins in the vineyard. One of the keys to obtaining a quality crop is to ensure that the grape variety, the rootstock, and the soil are well matched. The winemaker's preferred methods of cultivation—as regards vine density, pruning, canopy management, soil cultivation, and the age of the vines, for example—also influence the end result, as do the changing climatic conditions and the presence or absence of pests and diseases that make each vintage a new challenge.

Advances in enology have contributed to a better understanding—and therefore greater mastery—of the three main stages of wine production, namely vinification, maturation, and bottling. Better hygiene, for example, prevents a vinegary edge developing. It is increasingly rare for

wines to turn to vinegar. Another significant improvement has been the use of temperature regulation during wine production, which has made it possible to control the fermentation process.

Nowadays, winemakers also have the knowledge and the means at their disposal to compensate for any deficiencies in the grapes. With experience, they can produce good wine even in difficult vintages. Nevertheless, all these positive developments can just as easily be a step in the wrong direction if they lead to vinification being seen as nothing more than an industrial process. Each country takes a different view of such matters, and procedures that are allowed in some countries (such as aromatizing the wine with oak shavings) are prohibited in others. Agreement also needs to be reached over what constitutes a wine, a good wine, and a great wine.

According to the European Union definition, wine is a product "obtained exclusively by alcoholic fermentation, wholly or partially, of raw grapes, whether crushed or not, or of their must." In some parts of the world, however, drinks made from other fruits may also be called "wine." Beyond this, a distinction can be made between mass-produced wines and fine wines.

Left: The Gallo Winery's pressing plant in Sonoma, California
Center: Temperature-controlled stainless steel tanks
Right: Double-walled wine tanks in Somontano, Spain

Consumer product and work of art

When the modern wine industry in California and Australia was emerging, they resorted to imitation when it came to wine styles and labeling. They bottled "Burgundy," "Claret," "Champagne," and "Chablis" in particular, though it hardly ever involved Chardonnay. It was a state of affairs that became increasingly untenable with the growth in global trade. As their own growing regions still had to develop a reputation, they switched direction to international premium varieties which they emblazoned on the labels. As a result, Cabernet Sauvignon, Merlot, Shiraz, and recently Pinot Noir, Chardonnay, and Sauvignon Blanc have all become the darlings of the international wine trade.

Many superb New World wines are still bottled as single-variety today. When this approach reached the mass market, this obvious idea was very appealing to consumers all over the world—and others besides. Producers in other countries also followed suit. Single-variety wines began to take over the shelves and are now a well-established, integral part of the product range. While this has meant that grape varieties have assumed a brand role, a number of large companies have managed, with the right marketing, to successfully sell their varietal ranges under their own labels.

Consumers expect a brand to offer consistent quality every time. Yet that is inherently anathema to wine, which can sometimes have a widely divergent taste profile in terms of structure and concentration, depending on the location, microclimate, and seasonal conditions. So the wine industry and wine technology have made it their business to minimize these differences. At the same time it is about working in a way that is not only cost-effective, but above all profitable. The end product begins in the vineyard as well. So right from the start processes are geared to meet expectations, ensuring the price

Only maturation in barriques can refine the quality of well-structured red wines.

Fermentation of white wine in tuns—in this case Robert Weil's estate—helps to achieve top-quality.

level is set accordingly. The bargain that consumers always dream of does not exist in mass-produced wine.

And again, working towards high and maximum yields means that the grape quality of some growing regions leaves much to be desired, to varying degrees. This is where the winemaker's intervention comes into its own. On the basis of various analyses carried out as soon as the grapes are harvested, he or she knows what is lacking.

In the case of fine wine, the motivation is (ideally) quite different from the outset. The wine growers and winemakers in question regard their wine as a natural product which is a variable expression of its *terroir* from one year to the next. By this, they now see it as more than just climate, soil, direction, and grape variety, but as the philosophy and craft of the wine-

maker as well. The winemaker is concerned with exploiting the full individual potential and expression of the locality every year. Wine then becomes a creative process, like a work of art.

The lines are blurred, however. There are large-scale wineries with highly qualified winemakers who press excellent terroir wines alongside mass-produced ones; and well-known wine estates with outstanding crops which produce rather standardized, entry-level wines. But you also find winemakers who devote the same attention to all their wines. At the end of the day, wine consumers not only decide what they like, but also what approach they are encouraging as a consequence. Unfortunately they are not always aware of these processes.

Basic principles of

The amount of sugar in a must is determined by measuring its specific gravity (relative density). In the case of white musts, this is usually done before pressing. With red musts, a little liquid is drawn from the maceration or fermentation tank. The measurement is taken using must weight scales or a refractometer. Water, which has a density of 62.4 pounds per cubic foot at 39.2 °F (1 kg per liter at 4 °C), is used as a benchmark. The greater the amount of sugar in the must, the higher its specific gravity will be. The relationship between specific gravity, sugar concentration, and potential alcohol level is shown in tables. Producers work on the basis that

a white must needs 0.28 ounces of sugar per pint (17 grams per liter) to achieve an alcoholic strength of 1 percent vol, while red musts require 0.3 ounces per pint (18 grams per liter), because they contain a greater proportion of solids. In the case of red musts, the initial measurement is more problematic, because it is only carried out on the must that runs off when gentle pressure is applied.

Different countries use different systems of measurement and conversion, including grad, brix, baumé, and oechsle. The decision to enrich the must is made on the basis of specific gravity measurements, and again, different wine-producing regions

A drop of grape juice is placed on the glass of the refractometer.

The refractometer scale indicates the sugar content in the grapes.

winemaking

take different views. The grapes must have a minimum sugar content when they are picked, which in regions with appellations is laid down in regulations. This prevents harvesting beginning too early.

If the grapes are low in natural fructose, the situation can be improved to a greater or lesser degree. Special regulations have been introduced in some of the wine-producing regions. In each case, the legislation dictates the required minimum natural sugar content and the extent to which it may be increased. There are three methods of enriching the must:

- Adding sugar (chaptalization)
- Adding grape concentrate
- Concentrating the must.

In Europe, these methods are mutually exclusive. This is a regulatory restriction. There are no technical or qualitative reasons to prohibit their simultaneous use.

Grape concentrates have a higher sugar content than normal must and grape sugar may be added instead of sugar beet syrup or cane sugar. However, this affects the volume of the enriched harvest. European regulations do not allow the original volume to be increased by more than 11 percent, 8 percent, or 6.5 percent, depending on

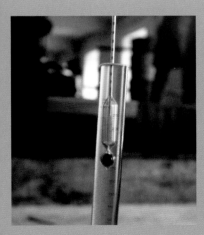

Traditional Oeschle scales are used to measure the weight of grape must.

Musts and young wines are repeatedly analyzed during the wine preparation process.

the region. With a traditional grape concentrate, all the components of the must are concentrated. Rectified concentrated grape must (R.C.G.M.) can also be used, which contains only sugar, the other components having been removed, principally by demineralization. Grape concentrate is denser than fermenting must, and it is important to homogenize the two during the enrichment process.

The newest enrichment technique is concentration, which involves removing a proportion of the water in the must. There are a number of ways of achieving this, including boiling it away, freezing the must and removing the lumps of ice as they form, and reverse osmosis. The latter is a filtering process: The must circulates along the filtration membrane, but does not penetrate it; a pressure differential allows only the water to get through.

The term "enrichment" encompasses a range of very different practices, and does not harm the quality of the wine, provided that certain rules are followed. It is a way of correcting a small deficiency in natural sugar, but will destroy the balance of the wine if overdone. Producers should always try to respect their raw material. Even the addition of grape concentrate can alter the original balance, which is why chaptalization is preferred in areas that have classed appellations.

Methods of concentrating the must alter the natural balance of the various components in the wine. As the volume of the liquid reduces, the proportion of solids increases, concentrating not only sugar, but also acids and immature tannins. Although these hi-tech methods are now widely used even in quality wine regions, they are in fact contributing to the continued standardization of wines, which cannot be in the interests of either the conscientious winemaker or the dedicated wine lover.

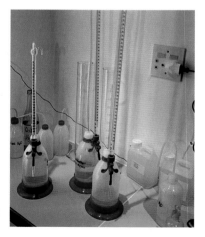

Many of the larger estates monitor and adjust levels of substances such as alcohol, acid, tannins, and residual sugar.

Chaptalization

Jean-Antoine Chaptal—the "inventor" of the enrichment process

Jean-Antoine Chaptal (1756–1832), Count of Chanteloup, was a trained chemist, and Minister of the Interior under Napoleon. Having published an influential article on wine in 1799, he wrote his famous work *L'Art de faire, de gouverner et de perfectionner le vin* (The art of winemaking) in 1807.

Although the process of chaptalization bears his name, he did not invent it. He was responsible for popularizing the method, however, which had been developed at the beginning of the 19th century, and involved adding cane sugar to compensate for any lack of ripeness in the grapes. Wine was enriched with honey in ancient times, and cane sugar was also used in the 18th century. Beet sugar did not appear on the scene until the second half of the 19th century.

Chaptalization is carried out by stirring cane or beet sugar into the must. The sugar is not tipped directly into the tank, because it would fall to the bottom without dissolving. Instead, the sugar is added to a quantity of must in a tub and stirred until it is completely dissolved. This mixture is then put back into the original tank.

Previously, chaptalization was usually carried out in a single procedure at the beginning of fermentation. Today, however, producers are altering their methods and spreading out the addition of sugar, especially in the case of red wine production. This enables the fermentation process (and thus the maceration time) to be extended without the risk of the wine developing a vinegary edge. The method is proving particularly interesting with grape varieties whose color is difficult to extract. The solids in the must of red grapes sometimes make it difficult to take any accurate measurements of must weight. In such cases, repeated chaptalization (usually twice) allows the producer to correct any errors in the original assessment and to control the enrichment process more accurately.

Chaptalization is required less frequently these days as a result of global warming, and also because winemakers favor lower alcohol content.

The balance of the wine

One key factor must be considered before winemaking: A wine's harmonious flavor is based on more than just its alcohol content; instead it is about the rounded balance of sweetness, alcohol, acidity, and tannins in particular. When tasting white or red wines, and dry or semi-sweet wines, the wine lover is judging this balance and harmony in the flavor. The wine grower or winemaker has to take account of this as soon as the grapes arrive in the winery.

Ideally, the grapes or must will already have an inherent natural balance which guarantees a good fermentation process and the satisfactory development of the wine. Unfortunately this is by no means always the case. Various factors can make the job of vinification more difficult. In cool regions, a bad year can mean that the grapes do not ripen fully and develop too little sugar: So they do not have enough potential alcohol and their acidity is too high and assertive. On the other hand, global warming and the pursuit of maximum phenolic maturity in red varieties leads (in regions that are already hot) to grapes with excessively high sugar levels which have lost most of their natural acidity in the process.

Either way, interventions are necessary in order to vinify an acceptable wine from the harvest. The first method will involve must enrichment (see page 89) and de-acidification, while the second involves dilution or alcohol reduction and the addition of acidity. The acids—tartaric, malic or citric, among others—are especially significant. The acid content not only has a

Well-ventilated clusters

small grapes

decisive influence on the subsequent flavor of the wine, as the acids also have a positive effect on the energy metabolism of the yeast during alcoholic fermentation. In addition, acids, and their salts are preservatives: They protect the wine from potential bacteriological changes, help to stabilize the wine, and contribute to its aging potential.

PARTIAL DE-ALCOHOLIZATION

High alcohol content achieved through heating and full maturity affects the balance of the wine, and can also present producers with financial problems if their wines are pushed into higher tax bands as a result. For this reason, wines are partially de-alcoholized in Australia and California using the spinning cone column, a rectification column with cone-shaped rotating shafts. The alcohol is only reduced in a small proportion of the overall amount of wine, and then blended back into the main part.

The problem of increased alcohol affects most wine-producing countries. Vineyard measures and spontaneous fermentation can lower the alcohol content slightly. Research is being conducted into yeasts which produce less alcohol yield than the standard commercial ones. Another effective way of reducing alcohol, and cheaper than the spinning cone column, is by reverse osmosis. Alcohol can be separated off along with water during the must enrichment process. This technique produces very balanced wines, provided there is good quality to begin with. Admittedly, this technical procedure is a controversial one.

and a low yield promise

a well-balanced wine.

Treading and pressing

Pressing takes place at different points in the winemaking process, depending on whether white or red wine is being produced. White wine grapes are generally pressed directly after being picked. The juice is sugary and sticky, which impedes run off and prolongs the pressing process. Fermentation takes place straight afterwards. During the production of red wine, the grapes or whole bunches are macerated and fermented before being pressed.

There are a number of pressing techniques. The choice of which one to use will depend on economics, the amount to be pressed, the type of wine to be produced, the available personnel, and possibly also the regulations in force in a particular region.

A TRIED AND TESTED SYSTEM

Wooden presses were used in ancient times, a fact proven by archeological finds and numerous accounts. The oldest surviving presses in France, Germany, Italy, and Spain are extremely impressive. Before the 19th century, only the nobility and the monasteries had their own presses. These were often imposing lever presses such as the one at Clos de Vougeot in the Côte d'Or. The growers paid a fee to have their

Historical table press: The grapes were spread on the table and weighted with the wooden lid, then the heavy central beam would be forced lower and lower using the two screws. This example is from La Rioja.

grapes pressed. After the French Revolution, smaller presses gradually caught on in the wineries.

The old presses had a horizontal trough into which the grape material or pomace was spread. In the case of lever or beam presses, one end of a heavy lever (formed by a long beam) squashed the grapes under a thick, heavy board. The other end of the lever was attached to a screw or spindle that raised or lowered the lever, depending on which way it was turned. Other wine presses had a central screw that pressed down on the boards forming the lid of the press. These devices did not retain the pomace at the edges, however, and so the lid had to be removed several times during the pressing operation, and the partially pressed grapes piled up again, until all the juice was extracted.

Improvements were made to this type of press over time. The grape material was held in place with baskets or grilles, the wooden screw was replaced with an iron one, and the screw-tightening system adapted to increase its efficiency and reduce the effort needed to operate it.

These hand-operated vertical presses were still in use in the 1960s, and can be seen in vine-growing villages and wineries today, where they often serve as decoration. The vertical principle continues to be employed in Champagne and other traditional regions although now, of course, the process is mechanically assisted.

A classic, relatively low basket press, still commonly found in the Champagne region, holds almost 4½ short tons (4,000 kg) of grapes, works gently, and produces high-quality must.

ADOPTING THE HORIZONTAL

Most producers now use horizontal presses, in which a press head forces the juice or wine through the perforated wall of a revolving cylinder. Changing the direction of rotation automatically loosens the cake of debris that forms. Provided that they are operated with the necessary sensitivity—meaning that only gentle pressure should be applied and the cake not broken up too often—presses of this type achieve very satisfactory results.

GENTLY DOES IT

Pneumatic presses constitute the latest stage in the development of the horizontal press. An airbag inside the cylinder is inflated, squeezing the must against the walls. The cake is broken up by slowly rotating the cylinder once the bag has deflated again. This is a much gentler system, and produces excellent results. A further advantage of this method is that small amounts can be pressed, whereas mechanical presses must be filled to a minimum level. This factor is very important in areas such as the Côte d'Or in Burgundy, where the large number of appellations

These pneumatic presses can be pushed directly under the emptying tank.

means that producers are generally dealing with very small quantities. There are also automated systems, called continuous presses, in which a continuous screw or conveyor belt transports the grapes through a cylinder, where they are subjected to increasing pressure. Belt presses squeeze the grapes between two perforated belts mounted one above the other, and are a little gentler than screw presses, which work like a large mincer. In both systems, the juice or wine runs off through the perforated walls. The free-run juice is collected at one end of the cylinder, and the press juice further to the rear. Once pressing is complete, the remaining pomace is usually filtered. These continuous systems can produce only medium quality wine at best, and this is why they are frowned upon in quality wine regions.

Two large, fixed pneumatic presses

A modern version of the old basket press

Alcoholic fermentation

During the fermentation process, sugar is turned into alcohol through the action of yeast, thereby releasing carbon dioxide and heat. Depending on the type of wine being produced, all the sugar may be fermented into alcohol to produce a dry wine, or only a portion may be fermented into alcohol, creating medium dry or sweet wines.

WHITE WINES

White musts obtained from pressing must be clarified before fermentation begins. The juice can be cleaned by removing suspended solids such as particles of soil and pieces of stem, grape skin, or other undesirable organic matter. The clarifying process is essential to the aromatic quality of the wine, but it must be used in moderation so as not to remove any of the vital material and thus prevent the must fermenting properly. If clarification is excessive, fermentation slows down, and may even cease altogether. The cloudiness of a must depends on the ripeness and health of the grapes. Overripe grapes heavily affected by rot will produce the cloudiest musts. All the mechanical processes to which the grapes are subjected, from harvesting through to pressing, contribute to the formation of solids, which is why such procedures should be kept to a minimum and be carried out as gently as possible.

Clarification can be static or dynamic.

Batonnage is the process of stirring fine lees.

In the former case, the must is left to stand in a tank for between 12 and 24 hours, to let the solids settle. The clear portion of the must, which may still contain some fine solids, is then separated from the coarse sediment. It is essential to ensure that fermentation does not begin during this period, because the bubbling would prevent the solids settling out. For this reason, the must is either kept at a low temperature or sulfur is added. The antioxidant sulfur dioxide has a further role to play, to the extent that it inhibits the growth of bacteria and wild yeasts.

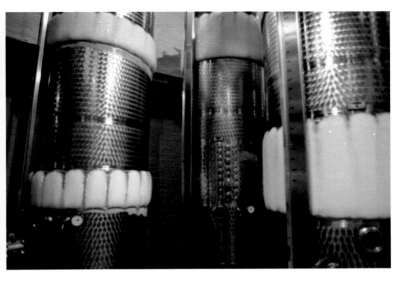

Above: Cooling tanks used for preliminary clarification or stabilization
Below: Fermentation at the ideal temperature in these computer-controlled tanks

Clarification can also be carried out dynamically—with the aid of a centrifuge, for example. Following clarification, the must can be fermented in a tank or in barrels.

The pros and cons

Selected yeast from a packet

Wherever grapes are grown, various types of yeast are also present. As soon as the skins of the grapes are damaged, these yeasts come into contact with the sweet juice. Some winemakers and enologists take the view that ambient yeasts are essential for a true expression of *terroir*. For this reason, more and more top winemakers are going back to spontaneous fermentation using the natural yeasts present in their vineyards and cellars. The same applies to winemakers who have switched to organic or biodynamic cultivation.

In conventional cultivation—when herbicides, pesticides, acaricides and insecticides are used in vineyards—a decrease in natural yeast populations can often be detected. The yeasts present are then, in some cases, unable to complete the fermentation properly.

Increasing numbers of winemakers prefer not to take any risks, and add commercially-produced yeasts, whose properties are known in detail. This can be done before fermentation begins, or used only as an initial boost where fermentation is slow or has been interrupted. Cultured yeasts come in the form of an industrially produced powder or granules, and are specifically chosen to fulfil a number of criteria. From a technical point of view, they must produce a significantly faster fermentation and a good output in terms of converting sugar into alcohol. If dry wines

MINNESOTA

MEGA MILLIONS

1373-035023875-190732

MEGAPLIER NO

001 06 09 39 50 64 MB 17 Q6

FRI FEB 19 21

$2.00

T11235900
01TXX%&% 02/19/21 13 42 23
R00112359 1373-035023875-190732

Check your ticket!
For winning numbers, go to
mnlottery.com or visit
any lottery retailer.

SIGNATURE _____

NAME _____

ADDRESS_____

CITY_____ STATE _____ ZIP_____

PHONE NO. _____

For your protection, we encourage you to always sign your ticket whenever presenting for payment or having it checked to determine winning status.

To claim your prize: Complete information above and sign. Prize amounts of less than $600 may be paid at any Lottery Retailer provided funds are available. Prize amounts of $600 or more require a claim form, which can be obtained from our website at www.mnlottery.com or by contacting the Lottery. All Lottery Offices will pay prizes up to $30,000, or the player may submit the ticket for payment by mail. Complete the ticket back, sign, and mail the ticket with a claim form to MINNESOTA STATE LOTTERY, P.O. BOX 131000, ROSEVILLE, MN 55113. Prizes over $30,000 must be claimed, in person, at Lottery Headquarters at 2645 Long Lake Road, Roseville, Minnesota.

Important: Tickets are bearer instruments until signed. All tickets, transactions, and winners are subject to the rules of the Minnesota State Lottery. Tickets are VOID if torn, altered, illegible, or incomplete. The Lottery is not responsible for lost or stolen tickets. **Website: www.mnlottery.com PH: 651-635-8273**

DDP REV. 02/08 Part# MN1000-01

| GAMBLING PROBLEM?
Call 1-800-333-HOPE
Not a winning numbers line. | CARE FOR
TICKETS: | Do not deface | Do not Iron | Avoid heat | Keep dry |

ZB247336554

SIGNATURE _____

NAME _____

ADDRESS_____

CITY_____ STATE _____ ZIP_____

PHONE NO. _____

For your protection, we encourage you to always sign your ticket whenever presenting for payment or having it checked to determine winning status.

To claim your prize: Complete information above and sign. Prize amounts of less than $600 may be paid at any Lottery Retailer provided funds are available. Prize amounts of $600 or more require a claim form, which can be obtained from our website at www.mnlottery.com or by contacting the Lottery. All Lottery Offices will pay prizes up to $30,000, or the player may submit the ticket for payment by mail. Complete the ticket back, sign, and mail the ticket with a claim form to MINNESOTA STATE LOTTERY, P.O. BOX 131000, ROSEVILLE, MN 55113. Prizes over $30,000 must be claimed, in person, at Lottery Headquarters at 2645 Long Lake Road, Roseville, Minnesota.

Important: Tickets are bearer instruments until signed. All tickets, transactions, and winners are subject to the rules of the Minnesota State Lottery. Tickets are VOID if torn, altered, illegible, or incomplete. The Lottery is not responsible for lost

MINNESOTA

The 2nd chance contests
for the holiday games end
soon. Enter your tickets
by Tuesday, February 23
for a chance to win cash
and lottery prize packs.
Details at mnlottery.com

1373-027333379-105432

001   03 13 25 29 35   Q5

FRI FEB 19 21

$1.00

T11235900
01MHJ3%S   02/19/21 13:42:22
R00112359 1373-027333379-105432

Check your ticket!
For winning numbers, go to
mnlottery.com or visit
any lottery retailer.

SIGNATURE _____

NAME _____

ADDRESS_____

CITY_____ STATE _____ ZIP_____

PHONE NO. _____

For your protection, we encourage you to always sign your ticket whenever presenti
for payment or having it checked to determine winning status.

To claim your prize: Complete information above and sign. Prize amounts of less than $6
may be paid at any Lottery Retailer provided funds are available. Prize amounts of $6
or more require a claim form, which can be obtained from our website at www.mnlottery.co
or by contacting the Lottery. All Lottery Offices will pay prizes up to $30,000, or the play
may submit the ticket for payment by mail. Complete the ticket back, sign, and mail the tick
with a claim form to MINNESOTA STATE LOTTERY, P.O. BOX 131000, ROSEVILLE, M
55113. Prizes over $30,000 must be claimed, in person, at Lottery Headquarters at 264
Long Lake Road, Roseville, Minnesota.

Important: Tickets are bearer instruments until signed. All tickets, transactions,
and winners are subject to the rules of the Minnesota State Lottery. Tickets are
VOID if torn, altered, illegible, or incomplete. The Lottery is not responsible for lost
or stolen tickets. **Website: www.mnlottery.com PH: 651-635-8273**

DDP REV. 02/08 Part# MN1000-0

GAMBLING PROBLEM?	CARE FOR				
Call 1-800-333-HOPE	TICKETS:	Do not deface	Do not Iron	Avoid heat	Keep dry
Not a winning numbers line.					

ZB247336552

SIGNATURE _____

NAME _____

ADDRESS_____

CITY_____ STATE _____ ZIP_____

PHONE NO. _____

For your protection, we encourage you to always sign your ticket whenever presenting
for payment or having it checked to determine winning status.

To claim your prize: Complete information above and sign. Prize amounts of less than $600
may be paid at any Lottery Retailer provided funds are available. Prize amounts of $600
or more require a claim form, which can be obtained from our website at www.mnlottery.com
or by contacting the Lottery. All Lottery Offices will pay prizes up to $30,000, or the player
may submit the ticket for payment by mail. Complete the ticket back, sign, and mail the ticket
with a claim form to MINNESOTA STATE LOTTERY, P.O. BOX 131000, ROSEVILLE, MN
55113. Prizes over $30,000 must be claimed, in person, at Lottery Headquarters at 2645
Long Lake Road, Roseville, Minnesota.

Important: Tickets are bearer instruments until signed. All tickets, transactions,
and winners are subject to the rules of the Minnesota State Lottery. Tickets are
VOID if torn, altered, illegible, or incomplete. The Lottery is not responsible for lost
or stolen tickets. **Website: www.mnlottery.com PH: 651-635-8273**

DDP REV. 02/08 Part# MN1000-01

GAMBLING PROBLEM?	CARE FOR				
Call 1-800-333-HOPE	TICKETS:	Do not deface	Do not Iron	Avoid heat	Keep dry
Not a winning numbers line.					

ZB247336553

# of cultured yeasts

are being made, the yeasts must have a high tolerance to alcohol, so that they can survive until fermentation is complete. Otherwise, there is a risk that fermentation would cease at between 11.5 and 12 percent vol, even though there was still sugar remaining in the must.

The yeasts are also selected with regard to their taste and smell. Generally speaking, neutral yeasts are preferable, because they do not affect the aromas of the wine. With certain grape varieties, however, strains that contribute to the development of a variety-specific aroma are chosen.

There is a danger that use of the same cultured yeasts the world over will lead to a standardization of wines. For this reason, an increasing number of wine-producing regions are selecting their own distinct strains. Nevertheless, many scientists hold the opinion that the raw material, i.e. the grapes, have considerably more influence on the eventual taste and aroma of a wine than the yeasts.

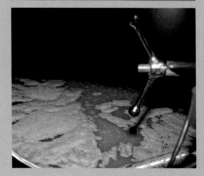

Adding acid and yeast cultures

Red wine vinification

Consideration should be given when vinifying red wine to tailoring the particular method to the grape variety and quality of the grapes, as well as the desired style of wine. Different procedures are required, depending on whether you want to produce a red wine for early consumption, or to obtain a wine that has the optimum aging potential.

The color of red wine is produced during maceration. During this process, phenolics, which include naturally occurring color compounds and tannins, and are found primarily in the skins of the grapes, are gradually extracted and begin to color the wine.

The alcoholic fermentation of red grapes takes place both in the liquid, or must, and also in the solid components—the skins, seeds, and stalks. To ensure satisfactory extraction of pigments and tannins, it is important to maximize contact between the solids and the liquid, otherwise the carbon dioxide that is released carries the solids to the surface, where they form a "cap." To bring the solids back into contact with the must, the fermenting liquid can be pumped from the bottom of the tank and released over the cap, a procedure called "pumping over" or *remontage*.

Another technique, known as *délestage*, involves draining all the must from the

tank so that the cap sinks to the bottom. The wine is then pumped back into the tank, completely submerging the cap and thus improving extraction. Alternatively, the cap can be manually or mechanically submerged using mixing paddles or poles, which is known as pigeage, or "punching down the cap." Extra pigments and tannins can be drawn out by extending the skin contact time. If the maceration time is too long, however, and continues after the alcoholic fermentation is complete, it can have decidedly negative consequences, because the wine is no longer protected from the oxygen in the air through the release of carbon dioxide.

Once fermentation is complete, the free-run wine is drawn off. The remaining solid matter, or whatever will not run off unaided, is pressed, and the resulting press wine can either be blended in immediately or finished off separately, depending on the desired type of wine. Press wine is considerably richer in tannins than free-run wine, and in general it is of lower quality. With wines made from grapes which are low in tannin, pressed wine will be added, while it tends to be omitted if the wines have a pronounced structure.

Left: Filling the tank with the mash
Center: Punching down the cap in a fermenting vat
Right: Stirring the cap in an open fermentation tank

Red wine in Burgundy

The great red wines of Burgundy are made exclusively from Pinot Noir, which is a challenging grape variety, particularly with regard to extracting the color. From the harvest onwards, therefore, producers try to avoid oxidation. The grapes are picked by hand, and are usually transported in crates. Any unwanted matter is then removed on the sorting table, or *table de tri*. The next step is the total or partial destemming of the grapes, depending on the grade of the appellation, the condition of the stalks, and the individual style of the winemaker.

In years when ripening the grapes has been difficult and the stalks are still green, they can all be removed. Some producers would rather destem the entire crop and

have longer maceration times. Others prefer to leave the stalks on a proportion of the grapes, particularly when producing wines for aging. There are advantages and disadvantages to both methods.

One of the golden rules is to minimize the use of pumps to move the grapes around, because they crush the stalks and seeds, which can give the wine a herbaceous edge and harsh, astringent tannins. Conveyor belts have proved to be a good way of transporting the grapes to the destemming machine or filling the fermentation tank. Sulfur is usually added at this point. An initial "pumping over" takes place, for the purposes of homogenization, and the levels of sugar and acid are measured for the first time.

The alcoholic fermentation then gets under way, with *pigeage* and *remontage* operations carried out every day. Once fermentation is complete, a few more days' maceration may be allowed. Carbon dioxide is no longer being produced, and so the cap gradually sinks. Caution is required if open tanks are being used, because there is a danger of a vinegary edge developing once fermentation is complete.

Emptying the tank starts with the wine being run off. The pomace is then pressed, and the free-run wine blended with some or all of the press wine. Next, the wine is clarified and transferred to barrels, where, sooner or later (depending on the vintage), malolactic fermentation begins. With a particularly acidic vintage, for example, this may not begin until spring.

Once the malolactic fermentation is finished, the first racking is carried out. The clear wine is separated from the sediment that has settled at the bottom of the barrel. The wine is exposed to the air during this process, to allow some of the carbonic acid with which it is saturated to be given off as carbon dioxide gas.

The wine is then transferred to another barrel for a period of maturation. Further racking may become necessary during this time, using either an oxidative or protective method, depending on the results of a tasting. In the case of Pinot Noir, however, there is a school of thought which prefers to leave the wine alone until bottling.

Left: Fermentation of whole grapes has a growing following.
Center: Bernhard Huber carrying out "pigeage" by submerging the cap
Right: The solid parts of the grape mash rise to the surface.

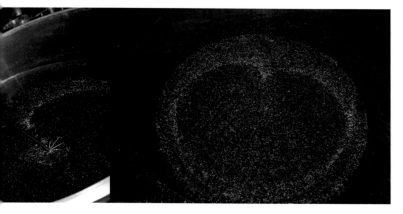

Carbonic maceration

One of the very oldest fermentation methods involved very little effort on the part of the winemaker. The grapes were picked and thrown into the fermentation vessel. In the beginning this was presumably no more than a cavity in the rock, then later amphorae or wooden vats. Some of the berries always break open when they fall in, and their must begins to ferment naturally, producing not only alcohol but carbon dioxide gas as well. Carbon dioxide is heavier than air, which is then gradually pushed out of the container. The lack of oxygen forces the remaining grapes to begin the so-called "intercellular fermentation" discovered by Louis Pasteur.

The natural enzymes in each individual berry begin the fermentation process, during which the grape must releases important color pigment and aromas from the skins, and a small amount of tannins. Then the formation of carbon dioxide during fermentation creates increasing pressure in the grapes until they burst and normal mash fermentation begins. If it is short in duration, the result is young, low-tannin wines ready for drinking, like those associated with Beaujolais or vino joven Rioja. This method is called *macération semi-carbonique* (semi-carbonic maceration). By extending the subsequent maceration period, however, it is possible to obtain very well-structured wines as well. This is known as "whole grape vinification."

The technique of pure carbonic maceration, or *macération carbonique*, was demonstrated as far back as 1875 by Pasteur, but it only enjoyed widespread application in the 1960s. It involves putting intact clusters of grapes into a fermentation tank pre-filled with carbon dioxide to create a high degree of intercellular fermentation. The process is designed to produce aromatic, fruity red wines with good colour but few tannins, which can be brought to market quickly. This method—initially used mainly for the Carignan grape variety in the south of France—has now spread to many other countries over the years.

Carbonic maceration involves the use of whole grapes in the fermentation tank.

Malolactic fermentation

Malolactic fermentation

This second fermentation converts malic acid to lactic acid with the aid of lactic bacteria, which may be naturally present in the winery or artificially added. As with alcoholic fermentation, the reaction is accompanied by the release of carbon dioxide, but in much smaller quantities. Malolactic fermentation alters the taste of the wine, and so is deliberately encouraged or specifically avoided. It reduces the wine's acid content, improves its aromas, and sometimes leads to a slight increase in volatile acids. The wine is made more stable, because there is no longer a danger that this second fermentation will take place in the bottle.

The lactic bacteria can also cause a decrease in other components of the wine besides malic acid. If they affect the sugars, for example, the taste may develop a lactic acid edge. Consequently, it is vital that all the sugar is broken down during the alcoholic fermentation. Sulfur dioxide added after pressing or to the tanks or barrels can render the bacteria inactive, without overly impairing the yeasts.

Most red wines undergo malolactic fermentation. Its use with whites and rosés depends on the region and the style of the wine. In regions with a Mediterranean-type climate, where the wines are often lacking in acidity, this second fermentation is avoided. In cooler regions, the wines tend to contain more acid, and so malolactic fermentation is often employed, provided that dry wines are being produced. If a wine contains residual sugar, chemical deacidification is used in preference to malolactic fermentation. In countries where there is no great tradition of producing sweet wines, this tends to be the practice with dry whites as well.

The perfect winery

"Assuming unlimited funds, describe your ideal winery." This could be a question from a viticultural exam or the title of an enologist's dissertation. Talk to any wine producer about the subject, and without exception, each one would give an answer reflecting the same priorities: the gravity principle, precise temperature control, equipment and rooms that are functional and easy to clean, and enough space for all the necessary tasks to be performed. Pleasing aesthetics should not be ignored, but rank below these on the wish list.

The ideal winery would be built against a hill, to allow ground level entrances, ideally on several floors. The top floor would serve as the reception point for the harvested grapes which would be loaded in crates. White grapes would be emptied onto a conveyor belt and gently transported to the press. The must would then flow into a tank on the floor below.

Red grapes would be tipped onto a slightly elevated *table de tri*, sorted, and then fed directly into a combined crushing and destemming machine at the end of the table. A movable sorting table and crusher-destemmer would enable workers to position the run-off point above the tank that is to be filled.

This very gentle process would transfer the white must and the red grapes to the floor below without the need for pumps. This is particularly important, because

Being able to work with gravity is a basic requirement for the perfect winery.

pumps crush the stalks of bunches that have not been destemmed, which can give the wine a herbaceous edge.

Once the white must had been clarified, it would run into tanks on the next floor down. Red wines would be fed into barrels, while the pomace would be removed from the tank and delivered to the press by conveyor belt. Racking would be carried out by using a pressure differential to "push" the wine from one vessel to another—a gentler method than pumping.

In this ideal three-story building, the barrique cellar would be on the lowest level, preferably underground, to make the most of the cool, constant temperature of the ground. The floor above would be at ground level, and house the fermentation hall and areas for bottling and labeling. The top floor, opening out onto the hill at the back of the building, also at ground level at this point, would be the reception point for the grape harvest. In reality, of course, it is rarely possible to come even remotely close to these perfect scenarios. Yet every winemaker and cellar master will try to optimize conditions in his or her own winery.

The ideal winery, therefore, should be in a position to handle both the grapes and the wine as gently as possible, maintaining the highest levels of hygiene and safety, while also operating in a way that is friendly to the environment.

The aging cellar is found in the basement.

The fully-automated winery

The ideal winery would not be fully automated, because winemakers like to retain control over the proceedings.

The only point on which they are almost all agreed is temperature control. The tanks are fitted with temperature probes and a double wall through which warm or cold water can circulate. The temperature in the individual tanks is displayed on an electronic control desk. Separate readings are given for each tank, because the must will not be at the same stage of fermentation in every one. The operator selects a suitable minimum and maximum temperature for each tank: the minimum temperature might be set at 68 °F (20 °C), for example, and the maximum at 95 °F (35 °C). As soon as one of these thresholds is reached, the computer can control the release of cold or warm water into the space between the walls.

With some tanks, it is possible to automate the task of "pumping over" (*remontage*), so that, for example, it can be set to take place every eight hours for half an hour. The frequency and duration of this process are usually decided by the winemaker after he or she has checked

Computer console to control the winery operations

the tank, then the operation is set to take place automatically. Pre-set machines can also be used for *pigeage*, or punching down the cap. They are mounted on rails above the tanks. Here too, however, the wine-maker will want to decide on the timing and duration. In reality, therefore, such systems can be considered a form of technical support rather than actual automation.

Automated tanks and pneumatic press

French oak forests

Since the 1990s, the demand for barriques—small oak barrels traditionally used in Bordeaux, usually with a 59-gallon (225-liter) capacity—has risen in leaps and bounds. In all the world's wine-producing countries, an ever-growing number of winemakers are choosing them as the vessels in which to vinify special white wines or mature their best reds. Oak from a number of countries is used to make barriques, but French oak is generally considered to be the finest raw material.

An oak tree takes 150 to 230 years to reach maturity and the stage when it can be used for timber. Consequently, sustainable, high-quality production can only be achieved by managing forests for the long

term. Controls on logging were imposed in France as early as the middle of the 17th century, in order to end the unregulated exploitation of the forests and guarantee a high-quality supply for future generations. As a result, France's oak forests are probably the finest in Europe today. The pedunculate oak (*Quercus robur*) and the sessile oak (*Quercus petraea*) account for more than one-third of France's 34 million acres (14 million ha) of woodland, and only a small proportion of this is allowed to be used for cooperage.

For a French oak, the route from the forest to the winery is a long one. The owner of the forest generally sells his trees to a forester before they have been cut down, and the forester then sees to the felling and commercial exploitation of the entire tree. The bark-covered stemwood used in the production of barrels is usually entrusted to a specialist timber merchant, the *merrandier*, who cuts it into *merrains*, the long lengths of wood from which the staves of the barrel are fashioned.

The production of stave wood requires a trunk that is free of defects, more than 16 inches (40 cm) in diameter, and can be divided into lengths of 43 inches (1.10 m)—the length of a stave. Of the 9.27 million acres (3.75 million ha) of oak woods in France, 4.5 million acres (1.85 million ha) are in public ownership

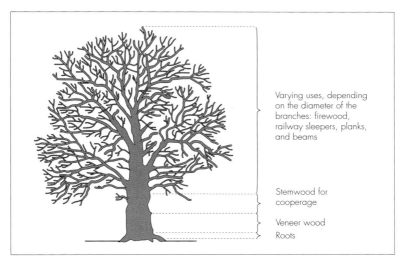

Varying uses, depending on the diameter of the branches: firewood, railway sleepers, planks, and beams

Stemwood for cooperage

Veneer wood

Roots

(as national forests or communal woodland) and are administered by the National Forestry Office (*Office National des Forêts*). The rest is privately owned. When a forest plantation reaches full maturity after about 200 years, only around 40 of the original 20,000 trees per acre (100 out of the original 50,000 per hectare) will still be standing.

The best wood is obtained from mature high forest trees. Younger oaks in a high forest often have defects, and tend to produce shorter logs. This kind of understory tree accounts for 90 percent of French oaks. Fully mature high forest timber is still relatively rare, and commands correspondingly high prices on the market.

Each year, the Forestry Office publishes a detailed list of the sections that have been released for sale in each forest, and marks the relevant trees. The lots are always sold as a complete unit. The coopers or their buyers inspect the area to be felled with all due care, and discuss things with the foresters. They assess each part of the trees and indicate whether they are interested in buying. The lots are sold in September and October at auctions with decreasing bids: A series of prices is announced, starting at a level suggested by the Forestry Office, and the first person to interrupt the bidding is awarded the lot.

The level of attendance at an auction will depend on the reputation that wood from a particular forest enjoys among winemakers. The sale in Tronçais, near Nevers in central France, is one of the more important dates on the calendar, as many coopers must have wood from this forest in stock if they wish to satisfy their customers. To secure their supply, they will often act directly as buyers.

Stave wood

Historically, a number of types of wood were used for wine barrels, including acacia, beech, poplar, chestnut, and cherry wood. Over the course of time, however, winemakers have discovered that only barrels made of oak or chestnut impart suitable aromas to the wines stored in them. Oak is the preferred choice, for two reasons: The aromas it contributes are far more interesting, and its properties best fulfil the cooper's technical requirements. Chestnut, however, is susceptible to woodworm, and is rarely used nowadays.

There are over 250 species belonging to the genus Quercus, but only three are important for cooperage. These are the sessile oak (*Quercus petraea*, synonym *Quercus sessiliflora*), the pedunculate oak (*Quercus robur*, synonym *Quercus pedunculata*), and the American white oak (*Quercus alba*). In French oak forests, sessile and pedunculate oaks usually stand side by side. The

two species are easily distinguished by their acorns: the acorns of a pedunculate oak develop on long stems (peduncles), whereas on a sessile oak, they are attached directly to the twig. In the forests of Limousin, pedunculate oaks predominate. The fact that competition from the understory is not very intense and the soil is fertile means that the wood is wide-grained, i.e. the distance between the annual growth rings is relatively great, because the spring growth, which lays down larger pores in the wood than the summer growth, is much more vigorous. In central France and the Allier region, where sessile oaks are the dominant species, poor soil fertility and competition among the trees impede annual growth, and so the wood is tight-grained and has smaller pores.

Research into the composition of the wood has shown that sessile oaks are richer in aromatic substances such as vanillin and methyl octalactone, whereas pedunculate oaks primarily contain phenolic compounds such as ellagitannins or catechol tannins.

Depending on the type of wine being vinified (white or red, with medium- or long-term aging potential, etc.), oak from a particular species or origin is preferred. There are no rules, however, and it is up to each winemaker to combine his or her own experience with the advice of the cooper. For this reason, winemakers tend to use barrels from various cooperages,

Many traditional wineries and châteaux once had their own cooperage workshops—nowadays frequently set up as museum exhibits—but few today still produce barrels themselves.

and also from different origins. The degree of chauffe (toasting) to which the barrels are subjected also has an influence on the aromas imparted to a wine as it matures. Wood from Limousin is largely used for brandy.

Precious staves

Both pedunculate and sessile oaks can be found in varying concentrations throughout Europe. A number of coopers have looked to the countries of eastern Europe to try to ensure a continued supply, but many of the forests they found there had suffered years of poor management. The Séguin-Moreau cooperage in the Charente has joined forces with Russian partners to build up an enterprise there; although the results are interesting in terms of flavor, Russian oak barrels are no better than French ones. Oak from Croatia has a good reputation, but there, too, stocks of high-quality stave wood are small.

American oak has been highly regarded for some time, not just on the American continent, but above all in Spain and Portugal, and more recently in South Africa and Australia as well. French winemakers and enologists have been more critical, complaining that its impact on the wine is too strong. Thanks to detailed research, American oak can now be employed in a more targeted fashion; its attractive price makes the decision even easier. Analyses have shown that American oak contains fewer tannins than French oak, but more aromatic compounds, particularly methyl octalactone. Barrels made from American oak need a long and heavy toasting during the production process, and are used for short periods of maturation (six to nine months at most), since their influence on the wine would otherwise become too dominant.

The choice of barrel remains an important decision for the winemaker, since it will have a considerable influence on the final quality of the wine. He or she must ensure that the aromas imparted by a particular barrel can be successfully integrated into the character of the wine.

The staves have to dry in the open air for two, preferably three, years.

Calculating the cost

To produce 35 cubic feet (1 m³) of stave wood, 176½ cubic feet (5 m³) of bark-covered stemwood is needed. The processing is done by the coopers themselves or left to specialist merrandiers. To ensure that the finished barrels are watertight, European oak wood must be split following the grain; therefore there is an extremely high degree of wastage. American oaks, by contrast, are denser and less porous, and can therefore be sawn without regard to the direction of the grain. This means that optimal usage is made of the wood, there is correspondingly little waste, and consequently, prices are lower. The economic return from barrel-making using American oak is around 50 percent, while with European oak the figure is only 20 to 25 percent. As a result, 35 cubic feet (1 m³) of staves from French oaks—enough to make about ten barrels—cost the equivalent of approximately 2,400 Euros at the time of writing, whereas the same amount of American oak can be bought for less than 1,200 Euros on average. To the price of materials must be added storage, manufacturing, and transport costs.

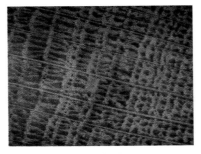

American white oak has the densest structure, and is easily made into barrels.

The wide-grained pedunculate oak is found in all French forests. Its wood is rich in tannins.

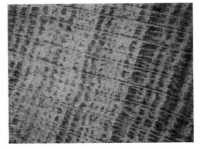

The tight-grained wood of the sessile oak is used for cooperage. It gives wine a note of vanilla.

Barrel

Before the logs go on to be processed, they are stored in the open air to leach out some of the tannins by exposing the wood to the elements.

Fortunately, the logs no longer have to be split with an axe, as special electrical cutting equipment now does the job.

The cooper uses a metal ring to hold the tapered staves as he begins to assemble the barrel.

When the circle is complete, the cooper secures it by hammering a second and then a third hoop around the barrel.

The cooper places a metal cable around the barrel and uses leverage to draw it progressively tighter, whilst also dampening the outside of the staves.

The staves are then brought together in a closed circle at the other end of the barrel, where they can be fastened with a hoop.

making

The barrel staves cut from the log are stored in layers in the open air again, where it takes three years for them to reach top quality.

The split wood is passed through a bandsaw so that the staves are equal in both length and width from the outset.

The staves are still splayed out at the other end of the barrel, and are heated over an open fire so that they can be bent to shape.

The intensity of this toasting is crucial in determining the aromas the finished barrel will impart to the wine.

The barrel does not yet have a side opening, so the cooper drills a bung-hole into the oak wood, countersinking it to the specified size.

The top and bottom may still have to be added, but the finishing touches are already being given to the outside of the barrel.

Barrel aging

There is no instant recipe for success in the art of turning grapes into wine, and the same is true of maturing the wine in barrels. The first decision each winemaker must make is the extent to which barrels should be used. In some cases, a proportion of the wine may be finished off in barrels, and the rest in tanks; the two are reintegrated directly before bottling to homogenize the blend.

For wine matured in barrels, especially new barriques, the origin of the wood, and the degree of toasting can emphasize particular characteristics in the wine that have been determined by the grape variety, weather conditions, and soil properties. As a rule of thumb, the more "structure" a wine has, the better it will withstand barrel aging. If a light wine is matured in a wooden barrel, all the care and effort that has been put into it up to that point can quickly be wasted.

As well as adding certain aromatic compounds, barrel aging allows slow oxidation, which encourages maturation. The various components of the wine combine with each other, making the wine more harmonious. At the same time, this controlled development makes the wine less perishable and more resistant to future oxidation—in short, it gives it greater aging potential. The additional oak tannins refine the tannins already present in red wine, and give whites a sophisticated tannic element that they previously did not possess.

Winemakers agree that the best way to achieve an appealing but integrated note of wood and more body in a white wine is to carry out the fermentation process in the barrel and then allow a period of maturation with the wine in contact with the lees. In this case, the must is transferred to the barrels after clarification. Once the alcoholic fermentation is complete, the barrel is topped up and the bung-hole sealed. The lees—the deposit left after fermentation—are stirred up periodically, a process known as bâtonnage. This ensures that the oxygen introduced into the barrel is carried right to the bottom, preventing the development of any faults in the aroma of the finished wine. How often the lees are stirred depends on the wine and the style of the winemaker. Initially, it may

Tartrates and fine deposits are removed from the barrels using water pressure.

Many distinguished estates have turned their barrique cellars into an architectural highlight.

happen twice a week, then gradually be reduced to once every two weeks. Whatever the frequency, it is generally continued for three months. After this time, the wine is either left on the lees or racked off. In the latter case, it may be transferred directly to another barrel, or the wine-maker may use the opportunity to blend the wine (the process of assemblage) before returning it to tanks or barrels.

Thirsty barrels

The duration of barrel aging varies from three to more than 18 months, and will depend on the type of wine being matured and the amount of volatile acid that forms in the barrel. If the level becomes too high, the period of barrel maturation is shortened. This decision is usually made by a taster, who is able to assess the general balance of the wine. A frequent mistake is to end barrel maturation too early, because the woody aromas that are often very prominent at the beginning need time to become smoother.

All barrels "drink" the wine, particularly new ones: The loss is estimated to amount to three to five percent. This means about 3 US gallons (11 liters) will disappear from a Bordeaux barrique with a 59-gallon (225-liter) capacity. The barrels cannot be left with an empty space inside, because a vinegary edge may develop in the wine. Consequently, they must regularly be topped up, a procedure known in French as *ouillage*. This occurs weekly at the beginning of the maturation period, and then at increasing intervals.

Barrel maturation, whether of red or white wine, is more labor intensive than aging the same volume in a tank. Add the cost of purchasing the barrels into the equation, and it is easy to see why it is so much more expensive. In deciding to use barrels, therefore, winemakers take into account not only the type of wine being produced, but also the final price. Only high-quality wine is worth carefully maturing in wood, to give it a harmony and complexity that it could never attain in a more neutral container.

The pipette, used to take samples from the barrels, is the winemaker's most important tool.

The winemaker checks how the wine is evolving through regular tasting and analysis.

Truth and illusion

Although aromatic compounds are absorbed during maturation in oak barrels, this is not "aromatizing" the wine in the true sense. Adding wood chips or installing wooden slats in stainless steel tanks is a different matter, however, because they have only one purpose: to impart aromas to the wine in the same way that seasonings are used with food. The positive secondary effects of barrel maturation, deriving from beneficial oxidation or contact with the lees, are not achieved with artificial additives.

The controversial use of wooden chips or slats in tanks is officially still banned in Europe, but properly registered experiments are permitted, and laboratories are already carrying out research and tests. Elsewhere in the world, this form of additive is widely used, and wines treated in such a way have long been sold across the globe. There is a problem with this winery practice: European legislation requires that any product labeled as wine is made entirely from grapes, a regulation that emphasizes the traditional precepts of purity. In an apparent effort to tailor products to the demands of the market, however, modern winemaking practice is resorting to a wide range of additional substances and aromatic compounds, even going as far as using specially manipulated cultured yeasts and a variety of enzymes. Should the consumer not claim the right to be informed about these additives, just as they are with other food and drink products?

Oak slats are a cheaper way of giving wine appealing oaky aromas.

Oak shavings give the illusion of being aged in casks to wines with toasted, vanilla aromas.

Clarifying and

As it matures, wine naturally becomes clearer and more limpid, but this self-clarification is seldom sufficient to guarantee the stability of the wine over a long period of time. For this reason, wineries make use of additional physical or chemical methods of purification. Such treatments must be carried out with great care, however, because if they are too harsh, they will diminish the wine and have a detrimental effect on its quality. A compromise has to be found between stability and structure. Moreover, stabilization should not prevent the further development of wines that are meant for bottle aging.

No clarifying procedure is suitable for all wines. An appropriate method must be selected, depending on the nature of the wine: red, white, or rosé, dry or with residual sugar, to be drunk young or matured, produced in bulk or for a small number of consumers.

Some great red wines should be bottled without any form of clarification, and the consumer suitably advised that a degree of sediment will form as the wine ages in the bottle.

Two methods of clarification that are usually used in conjunction with one another are fining and filtration. Fining is a physico-chemical process whereby an additive is poured into the wine which binds with the solids (such as proteins or tannins) that are making it cloudy, or are

In spite of various modern winemaking techniques, many top red wine producers rely on egg whites, a traditional fining agent involving a mild process.

The first stage of egg white fining is breaking the eggs and separating the whites from the yolks.

processing

likely to do so later on. The flocs formed settle out as sediment, and the clear wine can then be racked off. The choice of fining agent depends on the wine. Bentonite (a clay formed by the weathering of volcanic rock) and/or gelatin are preferred for white wines. With red wines, powdered or beaten egg whites are used as well as gelatin.

The fining process is sufficient to clarify some red wines, which can then be bottled. In most cases, however, it is carried out before filtration, in order to make the latter easier. Filtration is a mechanical process in which the wine is forced under pressure through porous material and the solids are left behind. The most

commonly used filters include precoat filters, sheet filters, and membrane filters.

The finer the filtration medium, the greater the stability of the wine, but the more it is stripped of its good qualities. For this reason, some winemakers offer connoisseurs unfiltered bottlings, in which the structure of the wine remains intact. The American wine critic Robert Parker has made a great contribution toward convincing both winemakers and consumers of the benefits of bottling red wines without fining and filtration.

Only the whites are used, and are stirred into each individual barrel of wine—a costly procedure.

The egg white binds with particles floating in the wine and sinks to the bottom, where it is drawn off.

Bottling

The equipment required for bottling depends on the size of the operation. Small estates often use manual bottling machines, in which the bottles are filled, one by one, and then corked using a second machine, again operated by hand. Other producers make use of commercial bottling services, whose equipment is usually technically impressive, guaranteeing the quality of the bottling process. Unfortunately, these commercial bottling services tend to lack flexibility, since their capacity—which can vary from 1,000 to 10,000 bottles an hour, depending on the size of the plant—must be booked in advance. In addition, the filtration carried out by bottling firms to indemnify themselves is often too harsh.

A bottling line consists of a washing unit to clean the empty bottles on the inside, a filling unit that fills the bottles to a preset level, and a corking machine. After filling, bottles can be topped with capsules straight away, labeled, packaged in cartons, and sent to a warehouse, from where they can be dispatched as required. Alternatively, they can be stored *tiré-bouché* ("filled and corked") in a wine cellar, from where they can be fetched when needed, cleaned, supplied with labels and capsules, and packed in cartons, which can then be sealed and piled on pallets for dispatch.

Modern automated bottling plant

Mobile bottling unit on a wine estate

Tartrates

Sometimes, particularly with white wines, small, hard crystals can be seen suspended in the wine or adhering to the cork. These look like sugar, but are, in fact, tartrates. Tartaric acid is naturally present in grapes, and thus also in wine. It crystallizes at low temperatures. To avoid this occurring in the bottle, winemakers can try to initiate the precipitation process while the wine is still in the tank or the barrel. This can happen naturally during the winter, if the temperature in the winery falls suf-

ficiently, or can be artificially induced by chilling the wine.

At the lower end of the quality hierarchy, heat treatment or pasteurization to remove microorganisms present in the wine and ensure clarity can also be considered. This process can be undertaken either before, during, or after the bottling process.

Bottles

The art of glassmaking seems to have been mastered by the Egyptians in the 4th millennium BC. It was the Phoenicians who disseminated both glass vessels and the knowledge of how to make them throughout the Mediterranean region. According to Pliny the Elder, Phoenician soda merchants were preparing their meal on a beach, and, lacking any stones with which to make a fireplace, they used lumps of soda, which then combined in the fire with the sand, producing soda glass. That particular story may belong to the realm of fable, but the discovery of one of the most versatile artificially manufactured materials used by man is indeed likely to have been a chance occurrence.

In addition to its decorative function, glass has always played a vital role in everyday life as a storage vessel, although in antiquity glass would certainly only have held valuable substances such as perfume oils. The fact that it could be made into almost any shape, blown, cut, bent, ground, and given almost any color, yet also melted down again at any time—recycled—led to the art of glass-making flourishing

Famous Château d'Yquem bottle signed by Thomas Jefferson

STANDARD SIZE RING
The standard neck ring takes a standard capsule and guarantees perfect corking.

A 20 °C NV 75cl ±1

GENEROUS SHOULDER
The broad shoulder gives an impression of class and elegance.

SLIGHTLY TAPERING BODY
The slightly tapering shape is reminiscent of the earlier Bordeaux bottles.

DEEP INDENTATION (PUNT)
This enables the bottle to be held securely in the horizontal position, making pouring the wine more pleasurable.

Measurements in millimeters

Traditional Bordeaux bottle

under the Romans, who popularized it throughout Europe. Glass furnaces have been found in all Roman provinces, and a few were undoubtedly still in use in the post-Roman era. For a long time, its fragility and the cost of production meant that glass remained the preserve of the wealthier sections of society (ordinary folk continued to carry and serve liquids in vessels made of clay, leather, or wood), but the triumph of glass was inevitable.

Balloon-shaped bottles appeared in the 16th century, with a wickerwork covering for protection. The use of bottles spread throughout Europe around the middle of the 17th century. Initially, they were relatively short, with a wide body and long, thin neck, but gradually evolved toward the shape we know today, principally to make it easier to store them on their side.

Design and tradition

Traditional wine bottle in different shapes

By the beginning of the 19th century, individual wine-producing regions were already using characteristic bottles, such as the flute bottle for Rhine wines, the bocksbeutel in Franconia (Franken), the straw-covered fiasco for Chianti, as well as the Burgundy, Bordeaux, and Champagne bottles, among many others. Since then, the catalogs of glass factories have continued to expand. Today, some appellations have typical bottles, and even large producers or merchants may use their own,

individual shapes. The current trend is to keep traditional bottle shapes for premium-category wines, that is to say, the heavy, more rounded body reminiscent of the late 19th-century style.

Italian bottlers caught the attention of the market with designer bottles. These are now used on an international scale, but seldom by the top producers.

Everyday wines are bottled in standard shapes, because economic considerations are of paramount importance. Technical advances have made it possible to manufacture bottles that are lighter and more durable than before, leading to important savings in transportation and glass recycling costs.

As the habits of consumers change, so glass manufacturers are adapting and becoming more imaginative. Most wine is sold in shops, where it has to compete with thousands of other products. The wines have to draw attention to themselves on the shelf, and so some producers go for a distinctive shape, others certain colors—both for bottles and for labels.

Bocksbeutel bottle dating back to 1893

too much, but a half bottle (12½ fl oz/ 37.5 cl) is too little. Consequently, bottles that contain 17 fl oz (50 cl) have been brought onto the market, but are only slowly gaining ground. The glass bottle is still the most commonly used container for drinks of every sort, although some wines are now being sold in plastic bottles or Tetra Pak cartons. Increasingly common is the "bag in a box" container, which consists of a plastic foil bag of wine (usually about 1–1¼ gallons/3–5 liters) inside a cardboard box. The bag collapses as the wine is drawn off, thus maintaining an almost airtight seal around the remaining contents. This kind of packaging looks set gradually to replace the sale of draft wine, because the "airless tapping" mechanism preserves the wine for a period of up to six months once the seal has been broken.

In the midst of all this innovation and creativity, however, it should not be forgotten that a wine is part of the tradition and culture of its country of origin, and this should be reflected in the design of the bottle.

We know that today's consumer is much more discerning and drinks less, but better quality wine. For some meals, particularly in restaurants, a whole 25 fl oz (75 cl) bottle may be

Substantial designer bottle for a Nero d'Avola

Bottle with a Châteauneuf-du-Pape brand seal

Bottle manufacturing

The main raw material for the production of glass bottles is silicic acid (silicon dioxide, 70 percent), which occurs in nature primarily in the form of quartz sand. An alkali is added (soda or potash, around 15 percent), which lowers the melting point to 2,732 °F (1,500 °C). Quicklime (10 percent) prevents the glass from crystallizing as it cools. The remaining 5 percent is mostly aluminum oxide, magnesium, or iron oxide, which primarily help to determine color and viscosity. Scrap glass (from manufacturing remnants or bottles collected for recycling) is also added. The amount of each ingredient is measured using electronic precision balances.

The mixture is melted down in a furnace at around 2,822 °F (1,550 °C). Bubbles of gas form in the molten glass at this stage, which rise to the surface and burst at 2,282 °F (1,250 °C) during what is known as the fining process. The now homogenous mass flows into channels which feed the molding machines. A plunger pushes the molten glass through a calibrated orifice at regular intervals. This produces a series of gobs of glass, which are cut off with automatic shears. Their weight, and hence the rhythm of the plunger, is determined by the amount of molten glass needed for the particular article being made. The temperature, now between 2,012 °F and 2,372 °F (1,100 °C and 1,300 °C), is constantly monitored, because a sudden sharp drop would cause the glass to lose its viscosity.

The molding process can now begin (see diagram, opposite). Each gob of molten glass drops into a parison mold. The lower part of this mold is a ring that shapes the upper part of the bottle neck. A plunger punches through the molten glass via the ring, and compressed air is blown in through the hole this creates, forming a hollow body from the gob.

This parison is transferred into a finishing mold, and compressed air is again introduced to give the bottle its final shape. This method of manufacture is known as the blow-and-blow technique. In the press-and-blow technique, the first blow molding operation is replaced by a pressing operation. Some machines can produce up to 700 bottles a minute.

Once molding is complete, the glass still has a temperature of 1,202 °F (650 °C). The external walls tend to cool off quickly, whilst the temperature inside the cavity drops much more slowly. If the bottles were allowed to cool naturally, the glass could develop cracks and easily break. For this reason, they are put through another furnace on a conveyor belt, so that they can cool off very gradually from around 1,022 °F (550 °C).

MANUFACTURING BOTTLES USING THE BLOW-AND-BLOW PROCESS

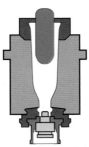

The molten gob of glass is dropped into the parison mold.

The lower part shapes the neck of the bottle.

Compressed air is forced in through a jet and blows the glass into shape.

The parison is transferred to a finishing mold, and another burst of compressed air forms the final bottle shape.

The bottles are put back into a furnace so that both the interior and the exterior reach the same temperature and can then cool off evenly.

Metal oxide vapors are sprayed onto the surface of the glass to remove any flaws.

A number of checks are carried out on the finished bottles.

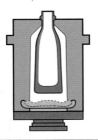

The wine-producing countries

Grape vines grow only in certain parts of the world. The key factor is climate, and more than anything it is the temperature that makes winegrowing possible, or not. Viticulture began its journey in the region around the Black Sea and the Mediterranean. Vines feel at home in regions where the thermometer climbs above 77 °F (25 °C) in summer, no matter which hemisphere. Another factor is the important part played by rainfall levels or drought. Winegrowing is a nonstarter if the annual rainfall is below 8 inches (200 mm), unless irrigation is an option. Yet too much precipitation limits viticulture as well.

Winegrowing spread from the Mediterranean to all the temperate zones of Europe. The great rivers with their moderating influence were the key players. Whether it is the Loire, Garonne, Rhine, Rhône, Danube, or Dniester, all of these rivers are arteries that supply the lifeblood to the major cultivation regions. A latitude of 52 degrees north used to be regarded as the northern boundary for winegrowing, but global warming has breached this boundary and viticulture is now possible even in the English Midlands, Denmark, Sweden, and Poland.

In North America winegrowing is sandwiched between the too high temperatures and aridity of the south and the too low temperatures and excessive rain of the north. The Pacific West Coast enjoys the most favorable conditions. In Asia vines are cultivated in the Hindu Kush mountain range, regions of India, the area around Beijing, and the northeast coast of China in particular, as well as in some parts of Japan. Winegrowing spread through the southern hemisphere in all regions where average temperatures do not fall below 59 °F (15 °C) in winter, and do not rise above 77 °F (25 °C) in summer: This applies to South America, South Africa, Australia, and New Zealand. The advantage in all these regions is that winemakers can rely on the grapes to ripen magnificently and the range of styles on offer is exciting and diverse.

Left: In northern Portugal grape vines are cultivated on narrow terraces above the river Douro.
Top: In Sonoma the temperate proximity of the Pacific has a positive effect on viticulture.

France

France continues to maintain its top position in the world of wine. Spain may have a greater cultivation area and Italy did in fact overtake France from 2007 to 2010 in terms of volume, but, according to statistics from the French government advisory agency Onivins, in 2011 France came second in terms of cultivation area with 2 million acres (807,000 ha), and first in production with about 1.3 billion gallons (49.6 billion hl) At the same time, champagne, Bordeaux, and Burgundy all come from France, three fixed stars in the wine production firmament: For the high quality is backed up by very significant volumes as well.

Around 600 BCE Greek settlers founded what is now Marseille and introduced vines. Then, from the second century BCE, Gallia Narbonensis (with today's Narbonne as its capital) was built up as a wine-producing province under the Romans. Viticulture soon began to develop in the Rhône Valley as well. Initially, Bordeaux—then Burdigala—was important only as a port for exporting wine, until vines were planted there, presumably in the 1st century CE.

Burgundy ("Bourgogne" in French) played a major role in winemaking during the Middle Ages—its monasteries of Cluny and Cîteaux, which were founded in 910 and 1098, were responsible for the promotion, refinement, and promulgation of viticulture. As part of Aquitaine (and therefore England), Bordeaux expanded its position as the key handling point for wine between 1152 and 1453. After the marshlands around Médoc were drained in the 17th century, Bordeaux developed as the source of elegant, light red wines extremely popular with the British—the clarets. Their prestige peaked for the first time in the 19th century, just as champagne began to take the markets by storm.

Winegrowing throughout France suffered a serious setback in the wake of the phylloxera disaster and the subsequent wine frauds and sales crises. Relief came in 1936 with the introduction of "Appellation d'Origine Contrôlée," a model system that undertook to guarantee the particular origin of the wines. A modern enology, or science of wines, emerged in the 1950s and, with it, a progressive form of viticulture. It meant that winegrowers and wineries in all the cultivation regions were then able to constantly improve the quality of their wines. The same approach is still taken today, with increasing emphasis on the *terroir*, sustainability, and organic viticulture in particular. Wines of unprecedented quality are being produced in the 400-plus appellation areas, known today as AOPs, as well as in the IGPs. As a result, France now produces the greatest number and diversity of internationally respected and sought-after top wines.

Opposite: Saint-Émilion is famous for well-balanced, elegant red wines.
Top: Champagne is the most northerly winegrowing region in France.
Center: Some of the best-known white wines come from Puligny-Montrachet.
Bottom: Séguret on the south bank of the Rhône is home to sun-kissed red wines.

ALSACE

Our overview of French wine regions begins with an exception. The ruling power has changed many times throughout Alsace's history, and as a result the region is characterized by a blend of Romance and Germanic cultures. Thus, basically, the same grape varieties predominate in Alsace as on the other side of the Rhine, around 90 percent of them white. The main ones are Riesling, Pinot Blanc, Gewürztraminer, and Pinot Gris, followed by Pinot Noir (the only red variety), Sylvaner, and Muscat.

Mostly single-variety vines are cultivated. The best wines come from 50 recognized *grand cru* locations. Many Alsace wines contain some residual sweetness. Regional specialties are the often outstanding sweet *vendange tardive* (late harvest) wines and the "Sélections de Grains Nobles" (from grapes affected by noble rot).

BURGUNDY

Viticulture flourished in the Burgundian monasteries of the Middle Ages. The limestone-clay and limestone-marl soils of the Côte d'Or are exceptionally variant-rich and each variety gives the wine different aromatic nuances. This diversity makes Burgundy fascinating, even though only two main grape varieties are grown there: white Chardonnay and red Pinot Noir. In the northern Chablis area, the Chardonnay grape develops a unique mineral content, while on the Côte de Beaune it acquires more volume and creaminess. In good years the Chardonnays of the Côte Chalonnaise come close to their expensive neighbors, while the Mâconnais subregion produces fruity whites. Côte de Nuits is the heartland of Pinot Noir, and its crowning glory, Chambertin. This delicate variety finds its most sophisticated expression here.

Hunawihr—eastern slopes of the Vosges mountains

Mercurey in Côte Chalonnaise

BEAUJOLAIS

In the Beaujolais region, extending from Mâcon almost as far as Lyon on the edge of the Saône Valley, the grape grown is almost exclusively Gamay Noir. The Beaujolais appellation yields fruity, palatable reds from the mainly marl soils in the southern half of the area. In Beaujolais-Villages, the region's center, the wine's appealing berry fruit has a slightly bolder structure. Both appellations produce Beaujolais Nouveau.

Crystalline rock predominates to the north of Villefranche-sur-Saône, especially weathered granite. The slopes there produce the ten Beaujolais *crus*: Brouilly, Côte de Brouilly, Régnié, Morgon, Chiroubles, Fleurie, Moulin-à-Vent, Chénas, Juliénas, and Saint-Amour. The Gamay variety develops different complex aromas in each case there, some of which have astonishing potential.

JURA & SAVOY

With only 4,500 acres (1,800 ha) of vineyards, Jura has bags of character. The vineyards extend over sunny slopes ranging from 800 to 1,500 feet (250–450 m) high. Chardonnay and Pinot Noir are cultivated here alongside local varieties Savagnin (for whites), Poulsard (for lighter reds), and Trousseau (for well-structured reds). The overall appellation is called Côtes du Jura, which incorporates three smaller ones— Arbois, Château-Chalon, and L'Étoile.

Most of the Savoy locations are found in the Rhône Valley between Lake Geneva and Lac du Bourget, as well as to the southeast of Chambéry and on the warm slopes of the Isère Valley. While the bland Jacquère grape predominates, the most charming wines are based on the white Roussette or Altesse, and the red Mondeuse.

Juliénas, a famous Beaujolais cru

The medieval castle ruins of Arlay

CHAMPAGNE

Champagne is a broad stretch of land with rolling hills to the east of Paris, extending over chalky subsoil. Its main centers are Reims and Épernay. The chalk base not only gives the wines finesse; it also makes it possible to build vast underground cellars for bottle fermentation and maturation.

Champagne is divided into five zones: Montagne de Reims, Vallée de la Marne, Côte des Blancs, Côte de Sézanne, and Côte des Bar in the Aube. Champagne as we know it today began to be developed after 1728. It was initially produced in sweet form, but in 1860 Madame Pommery created the first *brut*. Most champagne is made from Pinot Noir, Pinot Meunier, and Chardonnay from a wide range of locations in order to maintain the same taste profile.

THE LOIRE

The course of the river Loire, which runs for over 600 miles (1,000 km), forms the most extensive wine region in France and is split into seven areas. Pays Nantais is the home of Muscadet, while the Fiefs Vendéens lie directly south on the Atlantic coast. Anjou-Saumur, with its eponymous appellation, and the adjoining Touraine subregion to the east produce excellent dry and sweet crops of Chenin Blanc and top Cabernet Franc reds, as well as more basic wines. Around the city of Orléans there are three small appellations bearing this name. The often fabulous Sauvignon Blanc of Sancerre and Pouilly-Fumé are located in the center. Of the four appellations of the southern Loire in the foothills of the Massif Central, Gamay is the main player.

Young vineyard near the village of Œuilly, not far from the champagne center of Épernay

The Saumur caves were used not only as dwellings but also as perfect wine cellars.

BORDEAUX

With an area of 290,000 acres (117,000 ha), Bordeaux is the most famous and also the largest quality wine region in the world. Its outstanding reputation was established mainly through classification of the Médoc *grands crus* in 1855. The sweet Sauternes and Barsac wines also obtained their classification in the same year. Other areas such as Graves and Saint-Émilion followed later.

There are a total of 57 appellations in the Bordeaux, or Bordelais, region. Merlot occupies the top position with over three-fifths of the cultivation area, ahead of Cabernet-Sauvignon with a quarter and Cabernet Franc with a good tenth. The art of Bordeaux lies in the *assemblage*, or blending, which uses varying proportions of the different varieties according to the vintage. Sémillon dominates the whites, ahead of Sauvignon by at least half.

THE SOUTHWEST

The southwest, between Bordeaux, the western Pyrenees, and the Massif Central, is made up of a large number of winegrowing regions. While appellations near Bordeaux—such as Bergerac, Côtes de Duras, Côtes du Marmandais, and Buzet—use the same grape varieties as their famous neighbors, a whole range of individual varieties has been preserved in the appellations further afield. They constitute the special charm of the southwest, whether it is Jurançon with Gros and Petit Manseng, Madiran with Tannat, Cahors with Malbec, Fronton with Negrette, Gaillac with Durasor Len de l'El, and Marcillac with Fer Servadou.

Few people are aware that, even today, committed winemakers in all the appellations of the southwest continue to produce wine with their own distinctive character.

Pomerol, the famous appellation on the "right" side of the river Dordogne

The vineyards at Saint-Jean-Pied-de-Ports are one of the most spectacular spots in the Irouléguy region.

RHÔNE

The Rhône is divided into two regions. The smaller one to the north stretches from Vienne to Valence. Its red wines, based exclusively on Syrah grapes often growing on steep granite or slate slopes, are among the best in France; Hermitage and Côte Rôtie are fine examples. The whites made from Marsanne and Roussanne grapes, however, or the Condrieu made from Viognier, are also very classy.

South of Montélimar is home to Côtes du Rhône and Côtes du Rhône Villages. The main features are a Mediterranean climate and the Grenache Noir grape, which is superbly resistant to heat, wind, and drought. Winemakers usually supplement it with Syrah and Mourvèdre, but often with Carignan and Cinsault as well. The wines found here, such as Châteauneuf-du-Pape, Gigondas, and Vacqueyras, are packed with warmth and southern spices.

Tasting bar in Provence

Tain l'Hermitage on the northern Rhône

PROVENCE

The Provence wine region stretches from the Alpilles mountains as far as Nice. It consists of almost 74,000 acres (30,000 ha) of cultivation area, of which the Côtes de Provence appellation makes up over 57,000 acres (23,000 ha). Then come, in descending order of size, Coteaux d'Aix-en-Provence, Coteaux Varois, and Bandol, as well as the four smaller appellations, Les Baux de Provence, Cassis, Palette, and Bellet. Provence's successful development as a popular tourist destination has led its winemakers to specialize in rosé wine. It now represents 87 percent of the region's wine production, with red at just 9 percent and white at 4 percent.

CORSICA

Corsica is one of the world's oldest wine regions. Today 17,000 acres (7,000 ha) of grape vines are cultivated, 7,500 acres (3,000 ha) of which are allocated to the appellations. Apart from the fortified Muscat and a tenth of dry whites, especially Vermentinu, red varieties for the production of red wine and rosé are predominant. Specialties are the Sangiovese known locally as Nielluccio, and Sciacarello.

Lecchia domaine, Patrimonio

LANGUEDOC

Previously scorned for its mass production, the Languedoc region has undergone a radical restructuring process. On the one hand, it has focused since 1987 on producing modern country wine, often single-variety Pays d'Oc wines, now known as IGPs. On the other hand, high-profile appellations have been developed on the best high plateaus and hillside locations. With a total cultivation area of 600,000 acres (250,000 ha), there is a huge selection of different varieties and all sorts of wine styles: from dry white, rosé, and red wines to sparkling wines from Limoux and sweet Muscats. Its main appellations are Corbières, Languedoc, Minervois, Saint-Chinian, Fitou, and Faugères.

Maury, looking onto Corbières

ROUSSILLON

Although closely related to the Languedoc in terms of climate and grape varieties, the Catalan Roussillon region cultivates its differences. It produces 90 percent of all France's *vins doux naturels* (lightly fortified wines): Banyuls, Maury, Rivesaltes, and Muscat de Rivesaltes, which include some extremely complex wines. Now, however, excellent dry wines are also being pressed from Grenache and Carignan vines that are more than a hundred years old. Mourvèdre and Syrah are used to make reds as well, while Syrah is also a popular choice for rosés.

Domaine de Clovallon near Bédarieux

Italy

During the heyday of the Roman Empire wine enjoyed a golden age. The Romans promoted viticulture throughout their sphere of influence and demonstrated an extraordinary flair for finding the best locations. They also attached great importance to the wine trade. Wine was an established and highly valued part of social life. When the Western Roman Empire fell in CE 476, however, a lengthy decline in winegrowing in Italy followed: Even the commercial trading dynasties like the Antinoris and Frescobaldis, who had risen to prominence during the Middle Ages, were unable to reverse the trend. Not until the 19th century were magnificent red wines produced in Piedmont and Tuscany, initially for the elite but now to the delight of wine lovers.

As was the case in all Mediterranean countries, wine was part of the daily diet and little heed was paid to its quality. This all began to change in the 1970s. In Italy, too, innovative winemakers sought to unlock the potential of their vineyards. However, they had to follow the legal procedures in place at that time, such as very long periods of fermentation in wooden casks, even though these rules ran counter to more recent knowledge about winemaking and restricted them to an extremely limited varietal range. Winegrowers were determined to free themselves from these chains, and planted the varieties that interested them. Often, they aged them in new Italian barriques for far shorter periods of time, labeling them simply as vino di tavola: The Super Tuscans such as Sassicaia, Tignanello, and Ornellaia developed in this way.

It was the start of a revolution that would gradually grip the entire country. In Piedmont a new school also emerged, producing intensely fruity and delicately spiced Barolos and Barbarescos, and these soon became popular with an international clientele. While the cellars were the first to be modernized, a new approach soon followed in the vineyards as well. More and more attention was paid to the special locations in the classic regions. Then came the discovery of the extraordinary potential of native grape varieties. Regions that had previously produced only bulk wine now began to forge their own identities. This applied not just to the northeast and northwest but increasingly to the south as well, especially to Apulia and Sicily. As a result, Italy today has a fascinating wealth of extremely varied and often magnificent wines to offer.

Opposite: Approach to Poggio Istiano farm near Castiglione d'Orcia between Montalcino and Montepulciano. The Sangiovese-based red wines are produced here under the Orcia DOC.
Top: Treiso, one of the most important winegrowing municipalities in Alba
Center: Montepulciano is one of Tuscany's most attractive cities, with a rich cultural history and a long tradition of winemaking.
Bottom: The first snows on the Madonie mountains in Sicily show a striking contrast to the autumnal hues of newly planted Cabernet Sauvignon.

Piedmont and the Northwest

Some of the terraced slopes of the Cinque Terre can rightly claim to be the most beautiful vineyards in Italy. But the vineyards of Liguria, which are scattered around the Gulf of Genoa, produce only small quantities, especially of white wine, and very little of it is exported. This applies to the Aosta Valley in the Alps as well. White and red grapes ripen on the valley's terraced slopes, which lie at an altitude of up to 4,250 feet (1,300 meters), and, although the wines are extremely elegant, they seldom leave the region.

The *grands crus* of Piedmont are a different matter. DOCG Barolo and Barbaresco occupy top position in the Italian wine hierarchy, especially the single-estate wines. The best locations are on the Langhe slopes facing south and southwest, not far from Alba. The grape variety that gives it such high quality, Nebbiolo, is very difficult to cultivate, loves calcareous marl or sandstone, and needs plenty of heat to ripen its fine tannins. They give it the structure that allows it to age for decades. There are two schools among the wine aristocracy: traditionalists who work with rather long mash fermentation and lengthy aging in large wooden barrels, and modernists who swear by shorter vinification and maturation periods in new barriques. It has long since been proved that both approaches are capable of producing magnificent wines, and both camps have cautiously edged closer together.

Following in the successful footsteps of the two big names, winegrowers have paid more attention to other grape varieties such as Barbera

The picturesque rocky coast of Cinque Terre

Barolo, the stronghold of Nebbiolo

and Dolcetto as well. Some of the success is also rubbing off on DOCGs from north Piedmont, especially Gattinara. The estates in Alba, Langhe, Roero, Asti, and Monferrato are being fired with even greater enthusiasm, and the aromatic Asti Spumante made from Moscato Bianco is enjoying its own international success.

Lombardy, of which the capital is Milan, produces a large number of wines, most of which have not yet distinguished themselves. Around Lake Iseo in Brescia province, however, Franciacorta has become the most prestigious region for sparkling wine, while the DOC Lugana on Lake Garda has made a name for itself with pleasantly dry white wines. In the Oltrepò Pavese growing area south of Milan, covering 42,000 acres (17,000 ha), the local sparkling wine has a long tradition, though the red wines made from Pinot Noir are attracting far more interest.

Ca' del Bosco in Franciacorta

The Northeast

Between the Alps and the Adriatic coast, the northwest vineyards of Italy vary widely in terms of geology and climate, ranging from mountains to lowlands. This is reflected in the wines, which fluctuate between high quality and bulk-produced, depending on whether the vines grow in stony soil or on fertile valley floors or plains.

TRENTINO

In Trentino viticulture extends from Lake Garda up through the valleys of the Adige River and its tributaries. The prominent grapes are Chardonnay and Pinot Grigio, which produce fruity, fresh white wines when they originate from the barren slopes. Many vines are cultivated on pergolas and high trellises, and often produce high yields. Cooperatives turn them into reasonably priced varietal wines, while sparkling wine producers use them to make attractive spumantes. The DOC Teroldego Rotaliano, a wonderfully complex red wine, is outstanding.

The famous Montan wine municipality in South Tyrol

SOUTH TYROL

Further up the Adige and Isarco Valleys lay the vineyards of South Tyrol, the Alto Adige. Since the 1980s the area's wine cooperatives and top winemakers have been battling it out in a healthy competition to see who can make the best wines from the best locations. Chardonnay, Sauvignon Blanc, Pinot Blanc, and Gewürztraminer have all been very successful, as have Pinot Noir, Cabernet, Merlot, and, last but not least, the excellent, richly spicy and original Lagrein. After years in decline, the Schiava grape—widely cultivated for Caldaro and Santa Maddalena wines—is experiencing something of a revival.

FRIULI–VENEZIA GIULIA

Viticulture takes place only in the southern part of Friuli–Venezia Giulia (Fruili, for short) but, where it does, it is extensive. Some of Italy's best white wines come from the DOC Collio on the Slovenian border, while Colli Orientali produces very

The Adige Valley in Trentino

intriguing reds made from distinctive local varieties. Winemakers make remarkable varietal wines from Friulano (previously known as Tocai) and Ribolla Gialla, as well as Pinot Grigio and Sauvignon Blanc. As in the case of the great DOC Grave di Friuli, the major successes have been with aromatic whites, decent Merlot, and Refosco.

Capriva del Friuli in Gorizia province

VENETO

Nearly one in five bottles of quality Italian wine comes from the Veneto. The province of Verona leads the way, with white Soave from Garganega and red Valpolicella, while the luscious Amarone is made from dried red grapes. In Veneto's other DOCs individual producers are the ones who deliver really high quality. The same applies to the region's top seller, Prosecco. Grapes from the variety of the same name go to make this popular light sparkling wine. Following a legislative amendment, the variety has been renamed Glera, and a distinction is made between DOCG Pros-

Gargagnago near Sant'Ambrogio di Valpolicella

ecco di Conegliano-Valdobbiadene and DOC Prosecco, which may also be produced in Fruili.

EMILIA ROMAGNA

Emilia Romagna, also part of the northeast region, together with its capital, Bologna, is famous for its rich cuisine, cheese, balsamic vinegar, and the sparkling red Lambrusco. The inhabitants are fond of effervescent wine, but these are rarely convincing. The best dry wines are made by individual producers in the Romagna area.

White wine Soave comes from the Veneto region.

Tuscany and Central Italy

Tuscany may well boast an ancient wine tradition, and the name Chianti has been used since the 13th century, but its true ascendancy really began in earnest only in the 1970s. It was a time when the influx of wealthy outsiders from northern Italy and other parts of the world brought fresh impetus to the region's viticulture. They acquired wine estates, hired the best enologists, invested in vineyards and cellars, and began to produce international-style wines, regardless of dusty old DOC regulations.

The newcomers exploited the potential of the hilly Chianti Classico region between Florence and Siena, with its soils composed of Alberese limestone and Gal-estro shale. It is here that ideal conditions for Sangiovese, as well as Cabernet Sauvignon and Merlot, are found—the last two, or blends using Sangiovese, give us the famous Super Tuscans. Despite the new regulations now in place, spicy Sangiovese with its fine tannins still dominates the DOCGs of the Chianti area and gives character to Italy's most popular quality wines.

To the south of Siena, Sangiovese is used to make the famous Brunello di Montalcino wine, which ages into a deliciously complex, spicy red. In nearby Montepulciano, as in Chianti, Sangiovese (also known locally as Prugnolo) is blended with other varieties to produce the floral, fruity Vino Nobile. On the coast the

San Gimignano: tall medieval towers and pleasant white wine

cult wine Sassicaia created interest in the gravel soils of Bolgheri, so now some great red wines come from this area as well as from farther south in Maremma. The most famous area there is Morellino di Scansano, where Sangiovese is the main player.

Olives are a second source of income for many winegrowers.

Tuscany produces only a few white wines of interest, with one exception being the DOC San Gimignano varietal white made from Vernaccia. One specialty is the dessert wine Vin Santo, which is made using dried grapes fermented for a long time; it is permitted to be produced in the Chianti area.

UMBRIA

Umbria is known for its Orvieto and Orvieto Classico, pleasantly drinkable white wines pressed from Trebbiano Toscano, Verdello, and Grechetto grapes. After Giorgio Lungarotti drew attention to Umbria's potential for red wine with Torgiano, Sagrantino di Montefalco became established as a full-bodied, spicy red.

Orvieto, the white wine region in Umbria

LAZIO

The Lazio wine region near Rome is home to Frascati, a wine that is as famous as it is simple. Only a small number of producers stand out, mainly for their red wines.

THE MARCHE

The Marche is a region of central Italy on the Adriatic coast. While the cooler climate of the hinterland supports fresh white wines like Verdicchio dei Castelli di Jesi, the most famous red, DOCG Rosso Conero, matures near Ascona. Based on the Montepulciano variety, it can achieve considerable quality.

Tenuta de Angelis estate in the Marche region

The South

Recently, the south of Italy and Sicily—for many years no more than suppliers of bulk wine to the wineries in the north—have gained a firm foothold in the wine market, though this does not apply to every region.

ABRUZZO

The Abruzzo region (capital L'Aquila) extends along the Adriatic coast as far as the area around the imposing Gran Sasso mountain. Grape vines grow on the sheltered slopes up to an altitude of 2,000 feet (600 meters), although they are also found near the coast as well. The simple white wines are made from Trebbiano d'Abruzzo, and the reds from Montepulciano d'Abruzzo. Unlike the whites, the reasonable, full-bodied red with soft tannins has won an extensive following. The potential of the small Molise region directly to the south has yet to be exploited.

The wine landscape typical of Abruzzo

PUGLIA

Comparable in size to Germany or South Africa with 260,000 acres (105,000 ha) of cultivation area, Puglia produces vast

A typical "trullo" near Locorotondo in Puglia

quantities of unremarkable wine on its fertile plains and rolling hills. A number of committed wine companies, however, are achieving international recognition with wines made from native varieties such as Negroamaro and Primitivo. Consequently, some of the more than two dozen DOCs have become household names, such as Primitivo di Manduria, Salice Salentino, or Leverano, as well as Castel del Monte made from the Uva di Troia red grape.

BASILICATA

In the mountainous region of Bari to the west of Puglia lies Basilicata. The slopes of Monte Vulture produce the punchy and intense DOCG Aglianico del Vulture, one of Italy's best red wines.

CALABRIA

Located on the "toe" of Italy, Calabria is home to the Gaglioppo grape, which adds dimension to full-bodied red wines, especially the DOC Cirò. Only a few estates in this hilly region yield convincing vintages.

Naples, the capital of Campania

CAMPANIA

The venerable wine region of Campania on the hills of the Tyrrhenian coast are having a hard time, in spite of boasting excellent varieties such as the red Aglianico (at its peak in the Taurasi DOCG) and the fascinating varietal whites, which were also awarded the highest DOCG status for Greco di Tufo and Fiano di Avellino.

View of Mount Etna from Taormina

SARDINIA

Sardinia has also preserved its own identity when it comes to wine, not least with the full-bodied Cannonau, the Garnacha (or Grenache) originally imported from Catalonia. The delightfully fresh Vermentino di Gallura is pressed on the northern tip of the island, while in the east Sella & Mosca produce decent cuvées from native varieties in the Alghero DOC area.

Tasca d'Almerita's Regaleali estate

SICILY

Sicily still conjures up images of the fortified sweet wine Marsala. With an area of 321,000 acres (130,000 ha) under cultivation, however, the island has now made a name for itself with its often outstanding dry white and red wines—mainly Nero d'Avola, but also Syrah, Merlot, and Cabernet. The Cerasuolo di Vittoria and Etna Rosso appellations are doing exciting work. In the hands of good winemakers, varieties such as the dominant Catarratto and Ansonica, Chardonnay, Pinot Grigio, Viognier, and even Grillo are producing pleasant, often astonishingly fresh whites. It is a sign that Sicilian winegrowers are proving to be a dynamic force in wine production.

Germany

The Mosel and Rhine regions owe systematic viticulture to the Romans. After Charlemagne, the Cistercian monks gave winegrowing a significant boost when they founded Eberbach Abbey in Rheingau in 1136 and introduced Pinot Noir, known locally as *Spätburgunder*. Riesling gradually became more important from the 15th century onward. During the 18th century this variety was planted on the Johannisberg estate in Geisenheim (Rheingau), and by 1775 growers there would allow noble rot to develop before harvesting. These fine, "noble" sweet Rieslings were among the most expensive and sought-after wines in the world at the end of the 19th century.

The disasters and world wars of the 20th century reduced and restricted German wine production considerably, and when confidence had been rebuilt in the 1950s, the majority of winegrowers concentrated on the mass production of sweetened wines. The introduction of the 1971 wine law did nothing to change this strategy. Since the 1980s, however, a few winegrowers have been inspired by the progress in enology in other wine-producing countries and have begun to aim for top quality. This trend, which accelerated in the 1990s, has once again turned Germany into an extremely interesting wine-producing country.

The northern location of the 13 growing areas means the wine styles differ from those in warmer regions—the grapes of both white (two-thirds of the 250,000 acres—100,000 ha—of cultivation area) and grape red varieties have higher acidity. In white wine it has to be balanced with some residual sugar, even in wines that are described as dry (up to 9 g/l). In sweet or fine sweet wines, the acidity balances out what can be a high natural sugar level, making the wine wonderfully light and giving it almost limitless aging potential.

The German varietal range has its own distinctive characteristics due to climate. Top position is held by Riesling, which is frost-resistant and high in quality. Second comes the early-ripening, high-yield Müller-Thurgau with its mild acidity, and then the red Pinot Noir and Dornfelder. Next are Silvaner, Pinot Gris, and Pinot Blanc (local names: *Grauer* and *Weißer Burgunder*, respectively), followed by a large number of insignificant varieties. The Pinot family in particular is increasingly popular with winegrowers and consumers alike. Higher-quality wines are usually matured in barriques, although results are not always convincing. The majority of wines produced in Germany may be simple and cheap, but the proportion of high-quality, great wines has taken a considerable leap.

Opposite: Bremm, south of Cochem, where the Mosel River forms a spectacular loop.
Top: Pinot Noir reaches full maturity on the slate slopes of the Ahr.
Center: Forst has some of the best wine locations in the Palatinate region.
Bottom: Ihringen is one of the most famous spots for wine in the Kaiserstuhl region.

MOSEL

The Mosel Rieslings are one of a kind. The steep slopes of the Cochem and Middle Mosel regions between Trier and Koblenz, with their blue Devonian slate and marly soils, together with the adjoining valleys of the Saar and Ruwer, produce wines with intense, often exotic fruity aromas and distinctly mineral notes. Their racy acidity makes them wonderfully vibrant and long lived. The noble sweet wines, in particular, have a rare balance and freshness with a very low alcohol content.

Winninger Uhlen, the prime location on the Mosel

AHR

Of all places, one of the most northerly cultivation areas, the Ahr region south of Bonn, is a stronghold of Pinot Noir and the early-ripening Pinot Noir Précoce varieties. The best winegrowers produce high-quality wines, especially from the slate and basalt soils of the sunny, steep vineyard slopes.

Bacharach, a popular wine town on the Rhine

MIDDLE RHINE

The small Middle Rhine region—with its castles, Lorelei rock, and the popular tourist destination of Bacharach—begins south of Koblenz. Riesling develops great finesse on the south-facing slopes and produces mainly medium-dry or sweet wines.

RHEINGAU

Covering around 80 percent of the cultivation area, Riesling has an even stronger presence in Rheingau. In the mostly deep, often calcareous soils of the right bank of the Rhine, to the west of Wiesbaden and

Marienthal Monastery on the Ahr

around Hochheim, the grape acquires a structure quite different from its Mosel neighbor: Bursting with fruit and extremely elegant, it produces some of the most famous Rieslings in the world. Slate predominates, however, in the hilly locations in the popular tourist town of Rüdesheim and in nearby Assmannshausen, which has specialized in Pinot Noir since 1108.

Marcobrunn, a single estate in Erbach, Rheingau

NAHE

The Nahe River, which joins the Rhine at Bingen, is a more complex region, with a wide spectrum of grape varieties including Silvaner, Pinot Blanc, and Pinot Gris. It is attracting a great deal of attention

Rotenfels rock on the Nahe River at Traisen

these days, thanks to the excellent, delicate Rieslings of its top winemakers.

RHEINHESSEN

The Rheinhessen region lies on the left bank of the Rhine between Bingen, Mainz, and Worms. With over one-quarter of Germany's total cultivation area, it is the largest production region and was formerly the main producer of several strong mass-export brands such as Liebfraumilch. Now, along with the Palatinate region, it has become extraordinarily dynamic. Young winemakers have made a name for them-

Wingertsheisjer in Westhofen

selves with some outstanding Rieslings and wines made from the Pinot varieties, rebranding Rheinhessen in the process.

HESSISCHE BERGSTRASSE

The Hessische Bergstrasse wine region lies between the western edge of the Odenwald forest and the Rhine. Comprising some 1,100 acres (450 ha) of cultivation area, its steep slopes yield a delightful Riesling low in acidity, while convincing Pinot is grown on the flatter locations. Nearly all of the wine produced is consumed within the region itself.

PALATINATE

The Palatinate, whose most southerly parts are warm enough to grow almonds and figs, is often referred to as the Tuscany of Germany. It is the second largest German winegrowing region, with just under a quarter of the cultivation area. Though Riesling is the leading grape variety, red varieties—including Pinot Noir, Dornfelder, Portugieser, and Saint Laurent—are also popular with winegrowers. Mittelhaardt, north of Neustadt, is famous for its top locations such as Ungeheuer and Pechstein. The southern Palatinate is beginning to raise its profile with excellent Pinot-based reds.

Burg Staufen in Breisgau

favorable conditions for their harvests of substantial Pinot Noir, Pinot Gris, and Pinot Blanc—all of which are excellent served with food. Almost half of the wines are vinified dry, often in barriques. Riesling plays a fairly minor role in this region.

WÜRTTEMBERG

The grapes of choice in Württemberg, where they are cultivated mainly in the Neckar Valley between Neckarsulm and

Birkweiler in south Palatinate

BADEN

The bulk of Baden cultivation extends for over 155 miles (250 km) along the Upper Rhine from Mannheim to Basel. Sheltered from the cold east winds by the Black Forest and from excess rain by the Vosges Mountains, Baden is the warmest region in Germany. Its winegrowers exploit these

Yburg Castle in a side valley of the Rems

Esslingen, are Trollinger and Lemberger. Two-thirds of all wines are red, and taking rosé into account this leaves just under 20 percent for white wines. Riesling stands out above the rest of the whites, in quantity as well as quality. The best reds are made from Lemberger and Pinot Noir, though Zweigelt or cask-aged cuvées using Merlot and Cabernet Sauvignon are exceptional.

FRANCONIA

The region's continental climate makes red wine the exception in Franconia. The dry, full-bodied Silvaner in its distinctive

Escherndorfer Lump in Franconia

rounded bottle known as a Bocksbeutel is also making a comeback and competing with Riesling, though Müller-Thurgau leads in terms of quantity. The famous slopes of the "Am Stein" winery rise above Würzburg with its charming architecture. Scattered farther up the Rhine are some more high-quality locations, such as Rander-sacker, Escherndorf, and Volkach, as well as on the edge of the Steigerwald nature reserve in Iphofen. Outstanding red wines are produced from Pinot Noir and Pinot Noir Précoce grapes in Bürgstadt.

THE EAST

Kloster Porta is the largest wine estate in the Saale-Unstrut region in the eastern part of Germany. What is now a regional winery was founded by Cistercian monks in 1066. Favorable climatic conditions keep rain levels low. The most convincing white grape varieties apart from Müller-Thurgau, which can be rather bland, are Pinot Blanc, Silvaner, and Riesling, while the reds are mostly from Dornfelder and Portugieser. In Saxony, wine production is concentrated in the Elbe Valley between Dresden and Meissen. Mainly Pinot Blanc and Gris, Riesling, and Scheurebe are grown on the very steep slopes, producing wines of high quality. Winegrowers have no problems with sales, as both regions are popular destinations for day trips.

The belvedere of Saxony's state winery

Central, Western, and Northern Europe

There is a general, and increasing, trend toward greater professionalization in the wine-producing countries of Central, Western, and Northern Europe. This is often reflected in precision use of cellar technology, while in the case of the most dedicated winemakers it can even manifest itself as a commitment to using as *little* technology as possible. However, this more professional approach is also evident in the scientific selection of the most suitable grape varieties or wine styles.

At the climatic limits of viticulture, in Denmark, Sweden, and Poland, winegrowers often go for varieties that are resistant to vine diseases and less susceptible to frost. To date, only a few wineries are producing volumes at a professional level. It is gradually dawning on producers in England that the climate and limestone soils are eminently suitable for making top-quality sparkling wines that can hold their own with a French champagne. As a result, many companies are increasing their cultivation of Chardonnay and Pinot Noir, and reducing still wine production.

In Luxemburg, producers rely on the established grape varieties that have proved themselves in the climate of the nearby Mosel. Winemakers are becoming more interested in St Laurent, which could supplement the meager range of red wine. Although the prevalent crop choice in Belgium and the Netherlands to date has been fine varieties like Chardonnay and Pinot Noir, and, specifically for sparkling wine, Sauvignon Blanc, Gamay, and Cabernet Franc, there is growing interest in varieties that are resistant to downy mildew.

The Swiss are their own wines' best customers, which sadly means that very few wineries are represented in the export market. Chasselas (known locally as Gutedel) is a popular, if normally rather uncomplicated, white grape; instead, the Swiss are recognizing the advantages of the international classics and producing ever-better Chardonnay, Sauvignon Blanc, Merlot, and Pinot Noir. The Valais canton is the only area where indigenous varieties are preferred and these do make some of the country's most interesting wines.

After the wine scandal of 1985, the Austrian wine industry dedicated itself to quality. There has been remarkable progress, but there are winemakers who are determined to push things further and who go to great lengths to bring out the character of their best locations and retain old vines. The international success of Grüner Veltliner has led to increased use of native grape varieties, especially Blauer Zweigelt, Blaufränkisch, and increasingly St Laurent as well. This approach should put Austria in a very good position for the future.

Opposite: Vineyards in Chamosan, Valais canton
Top: Wijnkasteel Genoels-Elderen estate in Belgium
Center: Limestone soils in Luxemburg
Bottom: Gamlitz, the largest winegrowing area in Styria

Switzerland

Switzerland has some 37,000 acres (15,000 ha) under vine in the area from Basel to Geneva, Liechtenstein, and Lugano. Most of the locations are actually on mountain slopes, as the topography is determined by the Alps and its foothills. This means that the vineyards are often fragmented, with some split over different valleys. This applies especially to eastern Switzerland, which is made up of small cultivation areas in the Schaffhausen, Thurgau, St Gallen, and Graubünden cantons. Hilly vineyards are found on both banks of Lake Zurich. Although the obvious crops are found—Riesling-Sylvaner (Müller-Thurgau), Chardonnay, Sauvignon, Pinot Gris, and other white varieties—Pinot Noir (Blauburgunder) merits special attention, in Graubünden at any rate.

Charming wines, known only to the initiated, are produced around the three lakes, Neuchâtel, Biel, and Morat. However, all three barely manage to scrape together 2,500 acres (1,000 ha), most of which is dominated by Pinot Noirs with bags of character and by some exceptional Chasselas.

Chasselas stands head and shoulders above the rest in the Vaud canton on Lake Geneva, where it also produces its most complex and distinctive wines. Very fruity reds are also blended from different grape varieties. In the flat vineyards of Geneva

The early 15th-century castle in Vufflens-le-Château is situated in the heart of top wine locations. Lake Geneva can be seen from its tower.

Vineyard parcels covering the slopes above the winegrowing village of Auvernier, with a panoramic view over Lake Neuchâtel.

canton on the other hand, winegrowers have specialized increasingly on red wine made from Gamay, Pinot Noir, and other varieties.

With 12,900 acres (5,200 ha) of vine, Valais has the largest cultivation area of all the cantons. Its south-facing terraces and slopes extend over the right bank of the Upper Rhône. The starting point for getting to know its wines are Fendant (made from Chasselas) and Dôle, a red cuvée made from Gamay, Pinot Noir, and up to one-fifth of other varieties. This Alpine region has raised its quality and reputation with, on the one hand, Pinot Noir and Malvoisie (Pinot Gris), Syrah and Ermitage (Marsanne), and, on the other, quite distinctive indigenous varieties such as Armigne and Petite Arvine (whites) and Cornalin and Humagne Rouge (reds).

The Ticino region in the far southeast corner of Switzerland has made a considerable breakthrough with Merlot, rather than with varieties from nearby Piedmont. It has been cultivated in Ticino since 1907.

Today it commands 80 percent of the 2,607 acres (1,055 ha) under vine in the canton, while only 208 acres (84 ha) are given over to white varieties. Merlot is mostly bottled as single varietals that range in style—depending on cultivation area, soils, and topography—from light and palatable through full-bodied and velvety and on to intensely complex. Some top winemakers are also experimenting successfully with other red varieties and cuveés.

Vines flourish on the spectacular terraces in Sion in the Upper Rhône Valley.

Around the picturesque little town of Riva San Vitale, and in Ticino canton generally, it is almost exclusively red grapes that are grown.

Austria

The history of viticulture on the river Danube and Lake Neusiedl certainly goes back a long way, but in 1784 Emperor Joseph II gave it a significant boost by decreeing that local wine taverns could legally sell their own wine. Crucially, he supported attempts to improve quality, which also became the main focus in the wake of the wine scandal in 1985, when a strict new wine law was introduced. Today the quality standards of Austrian wine are exemplary, and a large number of excellent winegrowers are producing wines with an international presence.

The style of the wines is heavily influenced by the convergence of the wine quarter's cool northern continental climate and the warm southern conditions of the Pannonian Plain. This is immediately evident in the famous cultivation areas along the Danube, around 60 miles (100 km) upriver from Vienna. Mainly on the weathered primary rock soils of its steep slopes, the Wachau Valley yields top-quality Riesling and Grüner Veltliner. Its competitors are the Krems Valley wines, where majestic, loess-based terraces follow a northeasterly route—a *terroir* favored by Veltliner. In the small valley of the Traisen River, winegrowers have focused on white wines, which are based on a diverse varietal range. The best Kamptal Rieslings ripen on the

The best wines in the Wachau region come from terraced vineyards, like the one seen here in Spitz.

Krems, the historical wine-producing town on the left bank of the Danube, is an ideal starting point to find out about the wine regions in the area.

slopes of the famous Heiligenstein volcanic rock formation, while elsewhere gravel and loess are the main soil types. Loess forms a layer up to some 65 feet (20 m) thick in nearby Wagram, which as a result is mainly known for its spicy, minerally Grüner Veltliner and Roter Veltliner.

Grüner Veltliner is also the dominant variety in the region, the largest cultivation area in Austria, with 33,000 acres (13,350 ha) under vine out of a total area of 108,330 acres (43,840 ha). Its expression here is fruity, peppery, fresh, and dry. To the east where it is warmer, there is more Pinot Noir and Traminer, especially in the highest-quality "Trockenbeerenauslese" category as well as in red wines.

Vienna is the only large city in the world with a significant winegrowing area of 1,512 acres (612 ha). Its "Wiener Gemischte Satz"—a mixed blend of different, mostly white, varieties from local vineyards—now has a good reputation, and some interesting reds are emerging as well.

South of the capital is the start of the aptly named Thermenregion (thermal region). Its specialties are Zierfandler and Rotgipfler whites, but as the climate is heavily influenced even here by the warm Pannonian Plain, many winegrowers also produce a range of convincing red wines.

Carnuntum, an even warmer neighboring region, has made a name for itself in red wine production. Its dense and stony clay and loess soils, interspersed with sand and gravel, yield excellent wines made from Zweigelt, Blaufränkisch, and St Laurent, as well as from Merlot, Cabernet Sauvignon, and Pinot Noir.

Nussberg, one of the most famous vineyards in Vienna, offers a fantastic view over the city and the Danube.

NEUSIEDLERSEE

"Neusiedlersee" refers to the most important winegrowing region about the north and east sides of Lake Neusiedl. A strip of outstanding red wine locations runs along its gently rolling slopes. In the 1980s many winegrowers concentrated initially on Merlot, Cabernet Sauvignon, and Syrah, but the picture has changed since then. Now they are focusing not just on Zweigelt, but on St Laurent and Blaufränkisch as well. When it comes to white wine the warm climate favors Pinot Blanc and Pinot Gris especially, as well as Chardonnay. The Seewinkel region produces fantastic specialty wines: Its vineyards enjoy the conditions needed for the production of noble sweet dessert wines.

NEUSIEDLERSEE-HÜGELLAND

This area with its double-barreled name stretches from the lake's west shore and the Leitha Mountains, extending further southwest to the Rosaliengebirge mountain range. The theme here is diversity—not only in soil types, but in grape varieties and wine styles as well. Just about everything can be found here: dry whites or reds, easy or demanding wines, and noble sweet dessert wines such as the legendary Ruster Ausbruch. The central subregion gives expression to the Leithaberg DAC (Districtus Austriae Controllatus: Austria's designation system), which comprises 19 municipalities. This area has a plethora of white varieties, while for red wine the emphasis is clearly on Blaufränkisch.

Some of the best Zweigelt, St Laurent, and Blaufränkisch grapes in Austria ripen in the northern part of Lake Neusiedl.

The Neusiedlersee-Hügelland region of Lake Neusiedl (Purbach pictured here) produces excellent red wines.

BURGENLAND

After the diversity around Lake Neusiedl, Mittelburgenland, with its main centers Neckenmarkt, Horitschon, and Deutschkreutz, seems far more homogeneous. Over 90 percent of the some 6,400 acres (2,600 ha) under vine specializes in red wine. It is known as "Blaufränkisch country" for good reason. This variety produces fabulously dense, dark reds with excellent tannic structure and fine acidity—wines that age magnificently. The heart of the small Südburgenland region is around Deutsch-Schützen and the Eisenberg hill. Blaufränkisch is impressive here as well, whether as a single varietal or in high-quality cuvées with Cabernet Sauvignon and Merlot.

STEIERMARK (STYRIA)

The region is dominated by the picturesque landscape of South Steiermark, with its 5,780 cares (2,340 ha) under vine and the largest number of top winemakers. The area's steeply sloped vineyards are spectacular. It is popular for its fruity, light, dry, and eminently quaffable white wines made from Welschriesling, Pinot Blanc, Chardonnay (known locally as Morillon for the past hundred years), Sauvignon (which grows extremely well), and other white varieties. In southeast Steiermark, with its scattered 3,200 acres (1,300 ha) of vineyards, fewer top winemakers offer the same varietal selection. West Steiermark is home to Schilcher, a rosé wine pressed from the Blauer Wildbacher grape.

Vineyards on the plateau above the major market and winegrowing town of Deutschkreutz, the heart of Blaufränkisch country.

A rattling klopotec, a picturesque windmill-like device used to scare off birds, has become the symbol of Styrian viticulture.

Spain

Despite the fact that its cultivation area has shrunk in the past decade by about half a million acres (200,000 ha) to 2.5 million acres (1 million ha), Spain is still the largest wine-producing country in the world. Yet it is by no means the biggest wine producer, in just third place after France and Italy with an average of 1 billion gallons (40 million hl). The reason is low yields. For one thing, many regions suffer from drought, which in some years can be extreme; added to which, the altitudes of this distinctly mountainous country carry substantial associated risks. In the center lie the extensive Castile plateau and its famous cultivation region, Ribera del Duero, where the vines grow at between 2,300 and 3,300 feet (700–1,000 m) above sea level and face the serious threat of frost in spring.

Even though vines were grown much earlier, it was the sea-trading Phoenicians who promoted viticulture in Andalusia from about 1100 BCE. Five hundred years later, the Greeks settled in Ampurias on the Catalan coast and continued the work of their predecessors. The Romans then took winegrowing to a higher level, as they did throughout their empire. The Moors tolerated viticulture, though it stagnated under their rule and suffered even greater setbacks during the Reconquista period.

The recovery began in the south. When Sir Francis Drake seized 2,900 casks of herry in Cadiz harbor in 1587, substantial amounts of Jerez and Málaga were already being exported. Two hundred years later, after the English had established their own bodegas in the region, the export trade would expand still further.

The modern era began in northern Spain in the mid-19th century, forcibly triggered by the mildew and phylloxera epidemics that decimated harvests in Bordeaux. Rioja changed over to barrel aging, initially producing imitative wine, but then going on to develop its own style, which is still a sure-fire success today. In Catalonia, Josep Raventós introduced bottle fermentation. He founded Codorníu in 1872, the first company in the country to produce cava, and this led to the emergence of a flourishing sparkling wine industry.

During the 20th century the trade and export of wine was paralyzed under the Franco dictatorship until 1975. Progress has been made only in the last 25 years. With aid from the Spanish government and the EU, cultivation practices have improved considerably and wineries have been updated. At the same time, Spanish winegrowers have put their trust in their established grape varieties and traditions, and the result is a very attractive wine portfolio. Today the Denominación de Origen (DO) appellations protect almost two-thirds of cultivation areas and wine production.

Opposite: Rioja Alavesa in the foothills of the Cantabrian mountains
Top: The art nouveau reception hall of Rondel (cava)
Center: Vineyard in Jerez, Andalusia
Bottom: Vines on the Ribera del Duero plateau

Vineyards of the Penedès region, famed for cava, extend over the foothills of the Montserrat mountains.

CATALONIA

Catalonians are known for their avant-garde tendencies. After all, the foundation was laid for cava production in Sant Sadurní d'Anoia, 30 miles (50 km) west of Barcelona, in 1862. This mainly involves using the native varieties Xarel·lo, Macabeo, and Parellada. Enologists and bodega owners in the Penedès region were the first to be amenable to French grape varieties, and as early as the 1970s they produced convincing branded still wines and top-quality cuvées. The Priorat region experienced its renaissance in the 1990s, securing a top position with red wines from the ancient Garnacha and Cariñena grapes.

ARAGON

In neighboring Aragon, Somontano in the foothills of the Pyrenees is something of an oddity. Although only a small region, the few winemakers are nonethless installing state-of-the-art technology in vineyards and wineries. In this way, they are making a name for themselves with appealing and aromatic modern wines.

Barren soils provide good conditions in Aragon (left) as well as in Castile and León (right).

RIOJA

In spite of major developments in Spanish viticulture, Rioja maintains its position as the most important and best-known region. Popular branded wines and a singularly diverse range of top-quality wines are being produced from over 155,000 acres (63,000 ha) under vine. Although there are now a large number of wineries that rely on their own vineyards, the majority of bodegas (including the biggest ones) source their grapes or wines to a great extent from winegrowers or cooperatives, and concentrate on maturation, blending, and marketing—a system that is very common throughout Spain. Many bodegas in Rioja and other regions continue to practice the traditional vinification methods used for Crianza, Reserva, and Gran Reserva. At the end of different aging periods, the wines are then bottled and marketed once they have reached drinking maturity.

CASTILE AND LEÓN

Rioja faces a serious challenge in the form of Ribera del Duero. The most famous DO region in Castile and León was a late starter. It was not until the 1980s that it attracted attention with its dense and exciting red wines made from Tinta del País (the local name for Tempranillo). The smaller DO areas of Toro and Cigales are definitely on a par, while Rueda, which is also on the Castile plateau, has made its mark with fresh white wines made from Verdejo and Sauvignon. In the far west of the region, DO Bierzo has raised its profile recently with its racy red wine from the Mencia grape.

Labastia in the Rioja Alavesa region

GALICIA

Apart from the DO Rias Baixas on the Atlantic coast—its Albariño is Spain's most elegant white wine—Galicia's other wines have remained largely unknown until now, despite the considerable potential of single varieties such as Godello coupled with a cool climate.

Terraced vineyards in the Rio Sil Valley, Galicia

CASTILE-LA MANCHA

Madrid is Spain's most important wine market, with its own DO comprising a cultivation area of around 30,000 acres (12,000 ha) that lies to the south of the capital. For a long time it produced only simple drinking wine, mainly from the white Malvar variety and red Garnacha and Tempranillo grapes. Bodegas there have raised their profile recently with well-made wines. Like the seven other DO areas, Madrid is part of Castile–La Mancha, the largest wine-growing region in the world with over 1.2 million acres (500,000 ha). The main variety is Airén, a resistant, if undistin-

Arenas de San Juan municipality in Cuidad Real

Windmills, the symbols of La Mancha.

guished, white grape. It is frequently used as the base for sparkling wine or else is distilled. Producers have been more successful with red wines made from Cencibel, the local Tempranillo grape, although Cabernet Sauvignon, Merlot, or Syrah are used as well. However, only Valdepeñas has managed to build a national and international reputation with its well-balanced, fairly light, and quaffable red Crianzas, Reservas, and Gran Reservas.

RIBERA DEL GUADIANA

DO Ribera del Guadiana, created in 1999, is made up of six cultivation areas with a total of 60,000 acres (25,000 ha) in the Extremadura region on the Portuguese border. Tempranillo is the main crop here, followed by Cabernet Sauvignon, although there is also a whole range of indigenous (mostly white) grape varieties. The best results have been with soft fruity red wines.

LEVANTE

The east coast of Spain and its hinterland, known as the Levante, is home to traditional winegrowing regions that some-

Utiel-Requena in Valencia province

imes struggle to keep pace with modern demand. This is true of Valencia, where he white Merseguera and Moscatel grapes eature strongly. By contrast, Utiel-Requena as Bobal, a red variety that is convincing when blended with Tempranillo and/or Cabernet Sauvignon. Moscatel has a ole to play in Alicante, though the red Monastrell is the main variety, used to make rosés and fruity reds.

MURCIA
Monastrell also calls the shots in the Murcia region. Bodegas in Jumilla and Yecla, n particular, are increasingly demonstrat-

The white albariza soils of Jerez

Yecla, the heartland of the Monastrell variety

ing its suitability not only for young wines but for great ones as well, either as a varietal or blended with Tempranillo, Cabernet, or Merlot.

ANDALUSIA
Andalusia is a whole subject in its own right when it comes to wine, for it is home to some of the most famous fortified wines in the world. Even though there is often less demand for them nowadays, you can still

find sensational, extremely complex, and sophisticated Finos, Amontillados, Olorosos, and Palo Cortados, whether from Montilla-Moriles, Condado de Huelva, or the famous "Sherry Triangle." Málaga has its own, very full-bodied, style of sweet wine. In Ronda, in the hinterland, some outstanding red wines are now being produced as well.

BALEARICS AND CANARIES
The wines of the Balearic and Canary Islands are real specialties, invariably pressed from indigenous grapes and full of character.

The Binigual Winery on Majorca

Portugal

Port wine is the first thing that springs to mind about Portugal. It still enjoys an excellent reputation and is an important part of the Portuguese wine economy. The country has experienced something of a wine revolution, however, and its portfolio of wines is both surprising and convincing, based on its potential as a winegrowing country and its modern approach.

The modern history of wine in Portugal began in the 12th century, when Cistercian monks founded more than a hundred monasteries and promoted viticulture after the Moors were driven out. At the end of the 14th century, after Portugal secured its independence from Castile for the first time, the wine trade with England began to flourish, albeit on the basis of acidic red wine from Monção and unfavorable conditions. These relations took on a more sig-nificant dimension when England imposed an embargo on French claret in the late 17th century. As a substitute was sought, the first sections of the Duoro Valley were terraced and planted with vines, although the trading side was firmly in the hands of the English. As a high-quality, fortified sweet wine, port wine owes its existence and huge success to the then Secretary of State (later made the Marquis de Pombal), who introduced stringent regulations for the production and trade of port, stipulating that only classified slate-based locations could be used.

Two other cultivation regions responded to the demand for sweet wines and founded their reputation on it. Beginning in the 15th century, Malvasia and other varieties were grown on Madeira. This island in the Atlantic developed into the ideal

The terraced landscape of Duoro is one of the most spectacular wine regions in the world.

supply station for English ships en route to North America, a move that boosted its sweet wine exports.

The chalky soils and proximity to the sea of the Setúbal Peninsula south of Lisbon proved the perfect location for Muscat, which had already risen to fame in the 17th century. While Madeira now cultivates its own wine styles and is modernizing, the Terras do Sado region, which includes Setúbal and Palmela, is currently finding success with exciting dry white wines and well-balanced reds.

Becoming part of the EU in 1986 has revolutionized Portugal's wine portfolio. Membership led to the dropping of the ban on small producers doing their own marketing, and this injected fresh impetus into the system. For one thing, international grape varieties were planted for dry wines, while consideration was also given to the great legacy of native grapes. Since then all regions have made substantial progress, and even winegrowers in

the Duoro region have grasped the new opportunities on offer, proving that their dry red wines can certainly come up to the quality standard of the famous port wines. Winegrowing in Portugal stretches from

Top: Steep vineyard terraces tower above the fishing village of Câmara de Lobos. The south coast is the most extensive wine-producing area in Madeira.

Quinta da Cerejeiras is decorated with the famous traditional blue tiles known as azulejos.

the Galician border in the north to the Algarve in the south. A total of around 620,000 acres (250,000 ha) are under vine, yielding on average 265 million gallons (10 million hl) of wine. The 11 Vinho regions stand out from the simple *vinho de mesa* (table wine), with brand-name wines as well as estate wines frequently appearing under their designations. Leading the way are the 29 areas of provenance that are recognized in the Denominação de Origem Controlada (DOC) category.

Grass sprouting between vine rows in Dão

BAIRRADA

South of Porto near the coast is Bairrada, one of the largest red wine regions in the country. In the past the wine was pressed almost exclusively from the Baga variety: When young, it is often rustic, tart, and heavy in tannins, although after years and even decades it develops remarkable elegance. Other varieties are now being cultivated for more modern wines.

Quinta de Côtto in Mesão Frio

VINHO VERDE

Vinho Verde—a light, slightly sparkling, white wine that goes well with seafood—comes exclusively from the green, humid northwest of the country. Its finest, more rounded expression is based on the Alvarinho grape. The red wine of the region with equally pronounced acidity has remained a local specialty.

Coimbra is popular with wine aficionados.

DAO

Dão also lies in the Vinho regional area of Beiras, which produces many interesting wines including sparkling varieties. Sheltered by a chain of hills and mountains, Dão is one of Portugal's largest red wine regions. The wines, which are based on native varieties such as Touriga Nacional, Tinta Roriz, und Alfrocheiro, have superb aging potential.

ESTREMADURA AND RIBATEJO

Estremadura and Ribatejo, north of Lisbon, are two cultivation areas that are fully

A fountain in Colares

exploiting the introduction of international varieties such as Chardonnay, Viognier, Syrah, and Cabernet. Today they produce a whole range of attractive white and red wines, which are now made with indigenous grapes as well. Among the traditional DOC regions, Bucelas is reviving its reputation with excellent whites made from

Arinto, while in DOC Alenquer many of the impressive historical quintas (country manors) are experiencing a renaissance as modern wineries.

ALENTEJO

The flagship of modern Portuguese wine, however, is Alentejo in the southeast hinterland, which has been described as the California of Portugal. Its hot, dry climate and barren soils provide the best natural conditions for mellow and robust red wines bursting with fruit. To achieve this, though, modern cellar technology with efficient temperature control is essential. Nothing daunted, numerous investors have carved out model estates in the vast, gently rolling hills of the region. Aragonez (Tempranillo) is leading the way over Trincadeira, although Syrah and Cabernet are also delivering impressive wines.

Derelict old windmills in Alentejo

Cork production

Portugal is the world's leading producer of cork. Its 1.8 million acres (735,000 ha) of cork oak forests represent 32 percent of the global cultivation area, ahead of Spain (22 percent), Algeria (18 percent), and Morocco (15 percent). Portugal produces 173,000 short tons (157,000 metric tons), which goes to make 52 percent of all the cork used in the world. In addition to its own production, the country imports cork as a raw material for processing. Spain comes way down in second place to Portugal in global production (29.5 percent), ahead of Italy (5.5 percent) and Algeria (5.2 percent). Northern countries also produce small quantities of cork, but Portuguese cork continues to enjoy the best reputation. Cork exports, especially bottle-stoppers, bring welcome sales revenue of nearly 700 million euros. Seventy-two percent of the cork oak forests are located in Alentejo, followed by Lisbon and the Tagus Valley (approximately 20 percent).

Traditional cork bottle-stoppers are cut from the bark of the cork oak (*Quercus suber*), a tree found predominantly in Mediterranean countries. It grows very slowly, forming a cork layer suitable for the manufacture of bottle-stoppers only after about 45 years. The harvest—also referred to as stripping, decorticating, or debarking—involves removing the bark as carefully as possible from the tree. The

Quercus suber, the cork oak tree

Stripping does not damage the tree

Outside surface of a plank

Cork structure of the plank's inner surface

Looking for the best place to punch

The punching process uses partly hand-operated machines

cork planks should remain largely intact so as to make processing easier. Equally, the tree must not sustain serious damage in the process, as otherwise the formation of cork during the next growth cycle would be hampered.

The first stripping of a cork oak tree is carried out when it is about 25 years old, and every nine years thereafter. The first harvests are used for the construction industry, especially for sound insulation. The cork planks usually remain in the forest for several months, allowing the tannins to oxidize and the tissue layer in direct contact with the trunk to dry. The planks are taken to the factory as required, where they are initially steeped in boiling water for one or two hours to kill microorganisms and insects, release tannins, and increase the material's density and elasticity, making subsequent work easier.

A second boiling process can take place after a resting period of one to two weeks. The planks are then sorted according to quality and thickness, cut into strips, and the stoppers are punched out in line with the grain of the trunk. This process can be done automatically, although the result is less satisfactory than if manually operated or if semiautomatic machines are used. Only a real person can choose the best place to punch out the corks.

Cork bottle-stoppers

Bottle-stoppers undergo a mechanical process: The ends are cut to the required size and the body is polished. This creates cork dust, which is collected and used to manufacture agglomerated cork.

The next step involves an initial automatic selection by machines that sort the stoppers according to the number of visible pores on the bark surface. The stoppers are then disinfected and washed. Fewer cork producers are using chlorine for this, as it can give the wine an unpleasant taint, and most producers are using peroxide instead. The required dosage and length of exposure time depends partly on the level of bleaching the customer wants. In some countries there is a preference for natural shades, while others favor very light stoppers. One or two drying processes ensure a moisture content of six to nine percent. The bottle-stoppers are then sorted once more.

Machines do the checking, but only of the stopper's body, not its ends. Then the stoppers are branded, using either a burning or ink method. This may involve

Cork taste

Like wine, cork is a natural product. For this reason there must always be an allowance for a certain error rate, and, despite every effort made by the cork producer, we occasionally come across a corked bottle of wine. The wine then has a very strong cork aroma, which usually intensifies through longer exposure to air. There are various reasons for this, though the most common are incorrect storage of the cork and insufficient disinfection.

Occasionally, the wine may not have a pronounced "corky" taste, but it fails to come up to its usual standard, or it has an off-flavor redolent of a cleaning cloth, mold, or the like. In this event, finding the culprit is not a straightforward process, as it can be caused by, for instance, the cork bottle-stopper, the bottling equipment settings, problems with hygiene conditions in the winery, or the storage conditions of the bottle-stoppers. As a result, the disappointed consumer blames the wine. For this reason, many winemakers are now opting for cork-free closures. Faced with this threat, European cork producers have drawn up a cork production charter and signed up to strict quality control.

personalized branding with the name of the winemaker, the winery, and/or the appellation, and possibly the vintage as well, or else a more general detail—it is entirely up to the customer.

The branding that a wine aficionado can expect to appear on the cork becomes increasingly precise in direct proportion to the quality of the wine, for the cork's specification should make it possible to pinpoint the identity of the wine—the cork, it should be remembered, usually outlives the label. During the final production stage, the cork surface is treated with silicon or paraffin, allowing the consumer to remove the stopper without too much effort.

1 Natural cork, low quality, 24 x 28 mm
2 Agglomerated cork, dyed, with two disks of natural cork, medium quality, 23 x 44 mm
3 Agglomerated cork, dyed, with two disks of natural cork; low quality, 23 x 40 mm
4 Natural cork, medium quality, 24 x 45 mm
5 Natural cork, medium quality, 24 x 28 mm
6 Natural cork, very low quality, 24 x 45 mm
7 Agglomerated cork, 25 x 38 mm
8 Natural cork, high quality, 24 x 54 mm
9 Synthetic cork
10 Champagne cork, high quality, 30 x 48 mm
11 Champagne cork, medium quality, 30.5 x 48 mm
12 Château d'Yquem 1945 cork

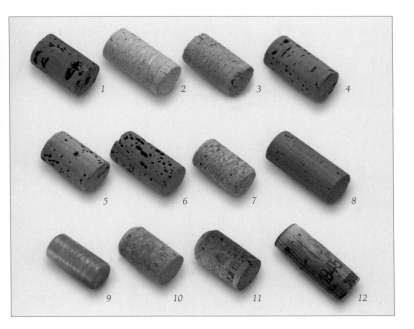

Central and Eastern Europe

Major transformations have taken place in the former Eastern Bloc, and not least in their wine industry. After decades of a state-controlled economy geared to mass production, private initiatives and international investment have now opened new doors. This applies especially to the countries that have joined the EU, such as the Czech Republic, Slovakia, Hungary, Romania, and Bulgaria. The reorientation of sales markets continues to be more difficult because exports to Eastern European countries have shrunk dramatically and are still limited in Western Europe.

HUNGARY

Hungary has a checkered history in relation to wine, which began with the Celts and then suffered bitter blows under the Mongols and Turks, followed by the phylloxera disaster. Under Communist rule, viticulture was expanded to 600,000 acres (250,000 ha) in the name of mass production. Only in the last 20 years has a restructuring taken place that is now delivering convincing quality. About half of the still-modest 160,000 acres (65,000 ha) of cultivation area is located on the Great Hungarian Plain, where mostly white wines and simple reds are produced. Around Lake Balaton they produce both still and sparkling whites, while reds with decent potential flourish in the Sopron region, especially in Villány in the south. Eger in the northeast is famous for its "Bull's Blood," now made mainly with Blaufränkisch. Tokaj-Hegyalja still leads the 22 winegrowing regions in Hungary, and the fine sweet dessert wine Tokaji (Tokay) is its flagship.

Opposite, top: Pezinok is an important winegrowing center in Slovakia, in the foothills of the Little Carpathians.
Opposite, left: Znojmo is the wine capital of South Moravia.
Opposite, right: Outstanding wines are produced in the area around Ormož in Slovenia.

Left: There are 57 wine press houses in Villánykövesd, a Hungarian village with 380 inhabitants.

SLOVAKIA

The 15 growing regions of Slovakia extend over 300 miles (500 km) along the border with Hungary and the Czech Republic. Four-fifths of approximately 64,000 acres (26,000 ha) consist of white grapes, including the main varieties Welschriesling, Grüner Veltliner, Müller-Thurgau, Pinot Blanc, and Feteasc. Red wines are pressed mainly from Blaufränkisch and St. Laurent.

CZECH REPUBLIC

Winegrowing in the Czech Republic is concentrated in Moravia, which sits on the border of the Austrian wine region. Less than 5 percent of the total 47,000 acres (19,000 ha) or so under vine are found in Bohemia. Most of the production is white wine made from Müller-Thurgau, Grüner Veltliner, Welschriesling, Riesling, Sauvignon, and Pinot Blanc, although there are also reds made from St. Laurent, Blaufränkisch, Zweigelt, Pinot Noir, and Cabernet. The quality is remarkable.

SLOVENIA

Slovenia has three major cultivation areas: Podravje, Posavje, and Primorska. Primorska borders on Italy and its Collio designation, and is internationally renowned for its excellent wines. In Podravje, Slovenia's Styria, the vines often grow on steep slopes. So far, Posavje, on the Croatian border, has barely managed to make its mark. Three-quarters of the 62,000 acres (25,000 ha) under vine are given over to white wine production while the other quarter yields some very convincing reds.

Melnik in southwest Bulgaria is synonymous with robust red wines.

BULGARIA

The Bulgarians were wise enough to exploit the fresh political start, adapting their wine production to meet international demand. They also invested in modern cellar technology when wineries and estates were privatized. The predominantly warm continental climate in the five major cultivation areas produces appealing red wines, especially since the introduction of Cabernet Sauvignon and Merlot back in the 1940s. A whole range of native varieties are also at the disposal of winemakers, but the state of the old vineyards is often lamentable. In recent years vineyards have been reduced in size by more than a fifth, to 180,000 acres (73,000 ha), although at the same time there is investment in new locations. Around 75 percent of the wines are now exported.

ROMANIA

Romania is one of Europe's major wine-producing countries, with almost half a million acres (200,000 ha) under vine.

Although the Carpathians are responsible for climatic variations, growing conditions are favorable. Moldova, the largest region (bordering the country of the same name), is home to the famous dessert wine Conair, as well as to dry whites and reds. Muntenia (Greater Wallachia) is renowned for red wines from its hilly locations planted with Cabernet, Merlot, Pinot Noir, and the

Young vineyards in Oprisor, Romania

indigenous Feteasc Neagr. Oltenia (Lesser Wallachia) is known for its medium-sweet wines, while white wine has been produced on the Transylvanian plateau since time immemorial. There is a plethora of native varieties, although export wines are based mainly on the international varieties.

MOLDOVA, UKRAINE, & RUSSIA

Wine has been grown since ancient times in the former Soviet republics on the Black Sea—Moldova, Ukraine, and Russia—but for many years huge quantities of bad wine

Vineyards at the foot of the Caucasus Mountains

were produced for consumption in the Soviet Union. Since the collapse of the Soviet Union, the wine industry has undergone a restructuring process, involving modernization through state initiatives and Western investment, and the quality of the wines has improved. As in the neighboring countries, there are still many native grape varieties but these are now supplemented by modern French varieties.

GEORGIA

Georgia is one of the oldest wine-producing countries in the world. During the Soviet regime large wineries were built here to produce vast quantities of medium-sweet red wine, mainly from Saperavi, for Soviet consumption. Under Gorbachev's anti-alcohol campaign and the 2006 embargo, nearly 170,000 acres (70,000 ha) of the 316,000 acres (128,000 ha) of vine were cleared. Today privately owned wineries produce wines mainly for the export market, made from indigenous varieties using modern methods. Traditional winemaking using kvevris (amphoras for fermenting and storing wine) is enjoying a renaissance and is arousing a great deal of interest in the West.

Grapes in Yalta used to make Crimean wine

Mediterranean countries

In ancient times grapes were cultivated in just about every country around the Mediterranean. Wine-filled amphoras were a widely traded and valuable commodity. The Phoenicians, Greeks, and Romans ensured the spread of viticulture, but a ban on wine consumption was introduced during the Islamic conquest of the southern and eastern Mediterranean. In all the Christian Mediterranean countries, on the other hand, wine was an integral part of the liturgy in the form of altar wine, as well as being part of the daily diet.

FROM CROATIA TO MACEDONIA

Wine was produced in Istria and Dalmatia on the Croatian coast a very long time ago. The main wines now enjoyed from Croatia's Mediterranean region are Merlot and the indigenous Plavac Mali, which is related to Zinfandel. Continental Croatia,

running from the Danube valley through Slavonia to the capital, Zagreb, is home to mostly white varieties. A total of some 150,000 acres (60,000 ha) are under vine.

Bosnia-Herzegovina lies immediately adjacent, on the Adriatic coast. The wine here comes for the most part from the karst landscape in the south of the country, near the city of Mostar. The two most impor-

Vineyards in Mediterranean countries often seem very old-fashioned.

Sveta Nedjelja, the picturesque wine village on the south coast of the Croatian island Hvar.

tant varietal names are Žilavka (white) and Blatina (red).

Serbia also has over 150,000 acres (60,000 ha) of cultivation area, divided into nine growing regions, and is far more important as a wine producer. Most of these areas are located near a river and have a continental climate in the north and a Mediterranean one in the south. Alongside the popular international varieties, the native grapes of greatest note are Smederevka and Neoplanta (whites) and Prokupac and Vranac (reds).

In the small town of Montenegro, influenced by the Mediterranean, the Plantaze winery has committed to high-quality vinification by installing the latest technology. It owns half of the total 10,000 acres (4,000 ha) of the country's vineyards.

In Macedonia, a poor agricultural country, viticulture is an important factor, with 55,000 acres (22,000 ha) under vine. Wineries and cellars strive to achieve quality here, too, and the red wines take precedence.

GREECE

In ancient times Greece had a huge impact on the spread of viticulture in the Mediterranean region. A new age dawned after the country joined the EU in 1981. Young Greek winemakers acquired their knowledge and skills in France and overseas. Subsidies allowed them to modernize the technology in their cellars and to plant new international varieties. At the same time, there was a growing awareness of the vastly diverse native grape varieties. They created a distinctive profile for Greek wines, either varietal or in cuvées, by using Assyrtiko, Vilana, Robóla, and Roditis (whites) and the red grapes Xynómavro, Agiorgitiko, Mandelaria, and Limnio, as well as Mavrodaphne for sweet wines. The growing regions with their Greek designations—27 OPAPs (Onomasia Proelefsis Anoteras Poiotitos) and 8 OPEs (Onomasia Proelefsis Eleghomeni)—cover mainland Greece and its islands. The wines may be still relatively unknown, but Greece is now delivering what are often truly great products.

Domaine Porto Carras on the Chalkidiki peninsula is among the largest and best wineries in Greece. Its vines grow on the slopes of Mount Meliton on the middle "finger," Sithonia.

Vines at the foot of Cappadocia's rocky peaks

TURKEY

With 1.2 million acres (500,000 ha) under vine, Turkey occupies fifth place in the global charts for cultivation area. However, vineyards are used primarily to produce table grapes and raisins. Only about 23 million gallons (900,000 hl) of wine are produced annually. Still, Turkish wine production is on the increase, in the very country that is regarded as a birthplace of wine. The European part of Turkey, Marmaris and East Thrace, accounts for two-fifths of wine production; another fifth comes from the Aegean coast, and nearly all the rest from central and southeast Anatolia. Special attention is paid to indigenous varieties. Large and medium-size wineries offer wines made to a remarkably professional level—mainly for tourists and Turkish restaurants abroad. There are now 38 wineries engaged in export production.

CYPRUS AND MALTA

Under Turkish rule, which began in the mid-16th century, viticulture in Cyprus ground to a halt and was revived only in 1878 under the British administration. The cultivation area on the Greek part of the island is now some 50,000 acres (20,000 ha). Apart from the famous Commandaria, a sweet dessert wine, some delightful dry wines are now produced by a growing number of independent wineries. Unlike Cyprus, winegrowing on Malta is fairly negligible, covering barely 1,200 acres (500 ha). The wine bottled on the island is made mainly from grapes or must imported from Italy.

Kthma Keo estate near Malia on Cyprus

LEBANON

Lebanon is one of the oldest winegrowing regions in the world. The temple of Bacchus in Baalbek, a city that flourished during Roman antiquity, is testament to the former significance of viticulture. The impetus for modern viticulture came from the Jesuits, who founded the Ksara winery in 1857 and introduced French varieties. Grapes cultivated on the slopes of the Bekaa Valley, at an altitude of 3,000 to 5,600 feet (900–1,700 m), ripen slowly and give incomparable balance to the wines.

Cupid at the grape harvest, Roman floor mosaic from El Djem, Tunisia

THE MAGHREB

In the Maghreb—that is, Tunisia, Algeria, and Morocco—the history of winegrowing dates back to the times of the Phoenicians. Even though the states are now predominantly Islamic, considerable quantities of wine are produced in the region. In Tunisia and Morocco, especially, French investment helped to improve viticulture and cellar technology, which explains the reliance on French grape varieties.

Vines planted in the Bekaa Valley

ISRAEL

Despite the ritual significance of wine in the Hebrew tradition, numerous references to wine in the Bible, and first attempts at winegrowing in the 19th century, Israel began to develop as a wine-producing country only in the 1980s. In addition to the large wineries, there are now a considerable number of small ones offering excellent wines made from international varieties.

Ancient winemaking facilities in Israel

South Africa

The first grapes were harvested on the Cape of Good Hope over 350 years ago, on February 2, 1659, by Jan van Riebeeck, the Commander of the Dutch East India Company. From then on, viticulture developed in fits and starts, although South Africa became an internationally respected wine-producing country only after democracy was established in 1994. Inroads were made in the production of quality wine in the 1980s, when high-grade grape varieties for dry wines were planted. Until that point the wine industry had been notable for its sweet fortified wines, its important brandy production, and by a quota system that imposed restrictions on all winegrowers.

When this system was abandoned, winegrowers on the Cape became incredi-bly dynamic because they could now plant what and where they wanted. Over 70 percent of the current total of in excess of 247,000 acres (100,000 ha) under vine has been replanted since 1994! In 1998 only 15.2 percent of production was red wine, and 84.8 percent what at that time

Franschhoek, renowned for its elegant wines and fine cuisine, proudly celebrates its Huguenot tradition.

Enclosed on three sides by picturesque mountains, Franschhoek is one of the most visited wine regions in South Africa

were rather unappealing whites; today reds represent 44.4 percent and whites 55.6 percent, so they seem to have found a desired balance. The leading grapes are still Chenin Blanc (18.2 percent) and Colombard (11.8 percent), ahead of Sauvignon Blanc (9.6 percent) and Chardonnay (8.1 percent), although some of the most intriguing white wines are now being produced from Chenin. As far as reds are concerned, Cabernet Sauvignon leads the way with 12 percent, ahead of Shiraz (10.3 percent), Pinotage (6.5 percent), and Merlot (6.4 percent).

There was also a shakeup in the structure of the wine industry. While there were still 4,786 primary wine producers in 1991, today's figure is only 3,527. In the same period, 70 cooperatives became 52 producer cellars, while the number of producing wholesalers that do their own vinification and bottling has increased to 25. The biggest change, however, has been in the emergence of privately owned companies. In 1991 there were 212 estates, mostly with 370 acres-plus (150 ha) under vine. Today there are 505 independent wineries, including 251 small-scale producers that process at most 110 short tons (100 metric tons) of grapes, that is, they own wine plots of fewer than 50 acres (20 ha). This small-scale structure has been a key contributory factor in improving the quality of the wines in recent years.

Buitenverwachting, in the now upmarket area of Constantia, is one of the oldest wine estates on the Cape.

Stellenbosch tops the league in South Africa in terms of the number of estates and the quality of its red wines.

THE CAPE WINELANDS

There may be important grape cultivation areas by the Orange and Vaal rivers in the hot, dry Northern Cape, but South Africa's main winegrowing region is concentrated in the Western Cape. The first vineyards were planted in Constantia in False Bay, which proved to be a remarkable choice. Constantia is a cool climate region with high rainfall levels and proximity to the Atlantic, conditions yielding fresh white wines and elegant reds, as well as South Africa's most famous wine, Vin de Constance, a sublimely sweet Muscat.

Stellenbosch—the second settlement on the Cape founded in 1679 by Governor Simon van der Stel—is the most famous wine region, as well as the largest. Its striking mountain ranges make it one of the world's most beautiful wine regions, and its weathered granite and shale terrain is home to some of the most ancient viticultural soils in the world. The region yields outstanding red wines in the form of either single-variety Cabernet Sauvignon or Bordeaux-style blends, as well as top-quality Shiraz and Pinotage. Viticulture also developed early on in the nearby Paarl region. Its distinctly Mediterranean climate produces mainly full-bodied, robust red wines, as do its Wellington and Voor Paardeberg "wards"—the name given to smaller independent wine areas. As the headquarters of the KWV (Koöperatieve Wijnbouwers Vereniging), originally a wine cooperative that controlled all of South Africa's viticulture during the twentieth century, Paarl was the country's real wine heartland. However, the wines of Franschhoek, a charming town settled by the French Huguenots in 1688, offer a far more diverse range.

Dornier in Stellenbosch—where art, wine, and cuisine meet

ON THE DYNAMIC FRINGES

Swartland, just an hour north of Cape Town, seems rather isolated. In recent years, however, it has attracted more attention thanks to Swartland Independent Producers (SIP), a group of mostly young winemakers who are producing fascinating wines from old, dry-farmed Bush Vines. Promising wine is also emerging from further east in Tulbagh, used primarily for white blends and convincing reds.

On the west coast, in Durbanville, Philadelphia, and Darling, the proximity of the Atlantic ensures cool temperatures, which are ideally suited to Sauvignon Blanc and stylish, elegant red wines. Similarly cool conditions are found southeast of Cape Town, where Elgin (South Africa's fruit-growing center) is making a name for itself with racy Sauvignon and Chardonnay, as well as reds with exceptional finesse. Since back in 1975 the cool maritime climate of

Walker Bay around Hermanus has been used to produce superb Chardonnays and Pinot Noirs. Even farther southeast, in Cape Agulhas, where the climate is also determined by the sea, the village of Elim made its mark initially with Sauvignon, and now impresses with Syrah as well.

Worcester, Breedekloof, and Robertson are warm growing areas in the Breede River valley. Decent, reasonably priced white and red wines are produced here, given sufficient irrigation. In Robertson, especially, an abundance of winemaking expertise is resulting in some outstanding wines.

Klein Karoo is a semiarid world all of its own, where viticulture is scattered around the villages of Barrydale, Ladismith, and Calitzdorp, which is the South African capital of port wine, a source of magnificent Cape Vintage Reserves and Cape Tawnies.

De Wetshof in Robertson

Aerial view of Calitzdorp

Asia

The wine-producing countries are paying ever closer attention to Asia. Hong Kong has established itself as the most significant location for wines at auction in the world, ahead of New York and London, since the local government made this its goal in 2007 and removed taxation on wine imports. From 2008 to 2012 the imported volume grew from 7.1 to 12.4 million gallons (270,000–470,000 hl), and the turnover from 340 million US dollars to almost 980 million, peaking in 2011 at 1.2 billion dollars. While nearly four in five bottles remain in Hong Kong, a good fifth is exported on. However, as far as wine consumption goes, China leads the way in Asia with 450 million gallons (17 million hl), far outstripping countries such as Japan, India, Singapore, Korea, and Thailand.

This puts China in fifth place globally, a trend that is increasing exponentially.

CHINA

Archaeological findings prove that wine made from grapes was produced as early as over four thousand years ago in the eastern Chinese province of Shandong. However, it was only under the Tang Dynasty

The showroom of Great Wall, the largest wine bottling company in China

Chateau Changyu-Castel is an impressive demonstration of China's ambitions in wine production.

in the seventh century that viticulture became more widespread. Modern winemaking was started by the Chinese diplomat Zhang Bishi, who founded Chateau Changyu in Shandong, imported dozens of *Vinifera* varieties, and built the large winery there. Today Changyu-Castel, which entered into a joint venture with the French Castel group in 2001, is China's biggest wine producer.

In recent decades China has steadily expanded its winegrowing areas. The 2012 report of the Organisation internationale de la vigne et du vin (OIV) recorded a 4-percent growth between 2007 and 2011—some 1.4 million acres (560,000 ha)—making China the fourth largest grape producer in the world. During this period, wine production increased by 6 percent to 348 million gallons (13.2 million hl), of which 90 percent was consumed by the home market. China now occupies sixth place ahead of Australia.

Winegrowing is made more difficult in China by what are in some cases extreme climatic conditions. Shandong, the main region lying between Beijing and Shanghai, suffers from heavy monsoon rains and severe frosts, as do the Yellow River valley, in Henan province, and the area around Beijing. Some of the grapes grown are native, resistant *Vitisamurensis* varieties. Since 1980 joint ventures with foreign (especially French) companies have accelerated the development of wine production and brought qualitative leaps.

Great Wall's main office is actually near the Great Wall of China.

Changyu Castel's vine plantings on the Hebei coast

INDIA

Even though traders are said to have introduced vines to India from Persia as early as 4,000 years BCE, actual wine production began with the Portuguese in their colony, Goa. Later, the British promoted winegrowing until phylloxera destroyed the vineyards. Given strong reservations about the consumption of alcohol, it took until the early 1980s for modern winemaking in India to get off the ground and for wine drinking to become popular among the burgeoning middle classes.

In 1982 Chateau Indage began to produce still and sparkling wines made from Chardonnay, Ugni Blanc, and Pinot Blanc and Noir, as well as from Cabernet Sauvignon, in the area between Puna and Nasik. Northeast of Mumbai, Nasik has emerged as the country's main growing region. The tropical climate makes large swathes of the subcontinent unsuitable for viticulture. Good conditions are found on hilly locations in Bangalore and in Himachal

Some of India's top white and red wines come from the Sula vineyards in Nashik and Dindori, some 110 miles (180 km) northeast of Mumbai.

Pradesh and Kashmir in northern India, although they have not yet been exploited on the whole. Today production stands at 3.4 million gallons (130,000 hl), and the trend is rising sharply. The potential of the Indian market is estimated at 30 million consumers.

JAPAN AND THE REST OF ASIA

In 1875 a merchant from Yamanashi, west of Tokyo, tried to produce wine commer-

Japan's indigenous grape variety Koshu is grown in the south part of the main island, Honshu.

Château Mercian's Jyonohira estate near the town of Katsunuma

cially, using old native grape varieties. He failed, but aroused interest in the process, and as a result *vinifera* and American grape vines were introduced. Producers only began to take a more professional approach to winemaking between 1950 and 1970, especially in Hokkaido and Yamanashi. For Japan's climate, with its extremely high humidity and icy winds in part, presents a major challenge to winemakers. In the 1990s the growing enthusiasm for wine in general gave something of a boost to Japanese viticulture. Alongside the drinks giants, many small companies are becoming actively involved in wine-making, and they have managed to substantially improve the quality and image of Japanese wines made from native grapes in the home market. Wine is now cultivated in Thailand and Vietnam as well.

Viticulture in a few Central and West Asian countries, such as Kazakhstan, Tajikistan, Uzbekistan, and Kyrgyzstan, has a tradition going back centuries, sometimes thousands of years. Grapes grown there are often Rkatsiteli and Saperavi (varieties well known in Georgia and Russia), as well as a wide range of other types, although in recent years the main focus has increasingly been on Western varieties.

North America

Dry Creek Valley near Healdsburg in Sonoma

The first attempts at winegrowing on the North American continent began not long after the arrival of the first European settlers. The south and west proved unproblematic, as the favorable climate there meant that vines introduced from Europe could be cultivated. In the early 17th century the Spanish planted their first vineyards in New Mexico and Texas. Then, in 1769, the Spanish royal house dispatched Franciscans to California to secure its territorial claims. The monks founded a total of 21 missions, the northernmost of which was Sonoma (founded 1823), and they introduced winegrowing in every location.

When gold was discovered near Sacramento in 1848, it unleashed the Gold Rush that enticed hundreds of thousands of prospectors to California, including winemakers from Europe. They soon realized there were more realistic prospects in viticulture than in prospecting. The next 30 years saw a substantial growth in winegrowing in California, until it, too, fell victim to the phylloxera outbreak in 1880. The 1920s Prohibition era proved a stumbling block to recovery, and winegrowers had to wait until the 1960s for a renaissance.

On the East Coast and in Canada viticulture had to surmount different obstacles. Attempts to plant the European *Vitis inifera* species were unsuccessful in the unsuitable climate, while the natives *Vitis labrusca* and *Vitis riparia*, along with newly developed hybrids, produced results that were not particularly palatable—consumed, at best, in the form of juice, sparkling wine, or sweet port and sherry imitations.

CANADA

The Canadian temperance movement meant that the moratorium on winery permits introduced in 1927 was not lifted until 1974. From then on modern viticulture was able to develop unhindered, leading to a new awareness of quality that was reflected in the introduction of the Vintners Quality Alliance appellation system in 1988. An extensive campaign of replanting with *Vitis vinifera* began, and it became obvious that the cooler climate could find expression in an appealing style of wine. Today Canada has a small but flourishing wine industry, producing around 15.9 million gallons (600,000 hl) annually, primarily for domestic consumption.

The country's two major winegrowing regions are south of Ontario in eastern Canada (especially the Niagara Peninsula) and the Okanagan Valley in British Columbia in the west, although there are winegrowing areas in Quebec and Nova Scotia as well. The best dry wines are now made from Chardonnay, Riesling, Pinot Gris, and Pinot Noir, although Merlot and the Cabernets feature, too. The grape of choice for Canada's specialty, its popular Icewine, is the hybrid Vidal.

The Okanagan Valley in British Columbia is by far the most promising cultivation area.

American Viticultural Areas

California may be America's largest cultivation area, but winegrowing is not restricted to just one state; grapes are grown throughout the US, even in Alaska, albeit to varying degrees.

EAST COAST

Winegrowing in New York State is incredibly dynamic, extending across the American Viticultural Areas (AVAs)—Lake Erie, Finger Lakes, Hudson River, and Long Island including the Hamptons. With some 11,000 acres (4,450 ha) under vine, Finger Lakes is the largest wine-producing area. Grape quality has greatly improved on the East Coast since the 1960s, thanks to the planting of French hybrids. Hybrids and the *Vitis labrusca* species are certainly still grown, but they have been planting *Vitis vinifera* for a long time as well, especially Chardonnay, Riesling, Gewürztraminer,

Sémillon, and Sauvignon Blanc, as well as Merlot, Cabernets Sauvignon and Franc, Gamay, and Pinot Noir.

In the New England states northeast of New York, some 40 companies are responsible for creating a vibrant winegrowing culture. New Jersey's vineyards are concentrated in the Delaware River valley, where the first winery was established in 1864.

Pinnacle Ridge Winery in Kutztown, Pennsylvania

Vineyards on Seneca Lake in the Finger Lakes cultivation area, the major wine region in New York State

Some of the cultivation areas in Pennsylvania and Ohio States are located around Lake Erie, although there are more extensive vineyards further south, to the east of Cincinnati in Ohio. There are over 110 wineries in both Ohio and Pennsylvania, which focus mainly on not only *labrusca* but increasingly *vinifera* varieties such as Chardonnay, Pinots Gris and Noir, and Cabernet Franc. Maryland's 450 acres (182 ha) under vine also yield interesting Chardonnays and Cabernets, as well as many other wines made from hybrids. The white wines from the East Coast are light and fruity, while some Chardonnays owe their toasted, caramel notes to oak barriques. Red wines are similar in style, although they are often marred by immature, vegetal notes.

THE MIDWEST

In America's Midwest, Michigan's wine-growing area is the main beneficiary of Lake Erie's temperate influence on climatic conditions. The vineyards cultivated by 100 wineries have doubled in the past ten years to just less than 2,700 acres (1,100 ha). Riesling is the most planted white variety, and Pinot Noir dominates the reds. Around 1,600 acres (650 ha) are now farmed by 115 wineries in the state of Missouri.

THE SOUTH

Viticulture also flourishes in a few Southern states, where wine tourism is very popular. In Virginia's 200 wineries, more *vinifera* vines than hybrids are grown, with Chardonnay and Bordeaux varieties emerging as the most convincing. European grapes also work well in Arkansas, North Carolina, and Georgia, whereas hybrids have produced the best results in Tennessee and Florida.

Bowers Harbor Vineyard in Traverse City on Lake Michigan

WASHINGTON

The climate in the northern West Coast of America is so damp that only very resistant, mostly white, grape varieties can thrive there. These conditions are typical of the Puget Sound near Seattle. Washington State is, however, home to excellent red and white wines, thanks to the cultivation area of the Columbia Valley. Sheltered from rain by the Cascade Mountains, healthy grapes grow here in an arid landscape that is suffused with light and irrigated sufficiently by the river. The severe frosts are the winegrower's biggest enemy, but growing conditions are so favorable that viticulture has taken a developmental leap, especially in recent years. Today 44,000 acres (17,800 ha) under vine yield the grapes for 740 wineries.

Their activities have led to 11 more being established in the overall American Viticultural Area (AVA) of the Columbia Valley: The oldest of these, Yakima Valley and Walla Walla Valley, are also the most famous. The key red varieties are Cabernet Sauvignon, Merlot, Syrah, and Cabernet Franc, which often reach world-class standard. Although Chardonnay is the dominant white variety, the best white wines are made from Sémillion and Sauvignon Blanc.

Walla Walla wine region on the Columbia River

OREGON

Although Oregon, with 20,000 acres (8,100 ha), is barely half the size of Washington and dwarfed by California, it has attracted the attention of wine lovers. It all began at a blind tasting, when the 1975 Pinot Noir from the Eyrie Vineyards in Willamette Valley beat prestigious Burgundies hands-down. In fact, the climate in the northern part of the valley is similar to the Burgundy region in France, a factor that proved a powerful draw for the more maverick members of the winemaking world. For the area had the potential to produce outstanding wines from Pinot Noir and Chardonnay, and Pinot Gris now as well, although the conditions presented a challenge and demanded huge personal commitment. As the different parts of the valley between the Cascade Mountains in the east and the coastal range in the west each develop wines with their own character, six sub-AVAs were created, including the most famous, Dundee Hills.

Southern Oregon—the Umpqua, Applegate, and Rogue Valleys, along with Oregon's slice of the Columbia Gorge in the northeast—is characterized by a warmer climate, so it is possible to grow Bordeaux and Rhône varieties with a considerable degree of success, as well as Italian and even Spanish grape varieties.

Willamette Valley is famous for its Pinot Noir.

California

The Pacific often provides the perfect climate for viticulture.

California is the viticultural giant of the United States. Almost 90 percent of all American wine comes from the "Golden State" on the Pacific Ocean.

CENTRAL VALLEY

The bulk of the wine comes from the Central Valley, mainly from its San Joaquin Valley, which is some 220 miles (350 km) long and over 55 miles (90 km) wide. In this hot, dry climate barely a quarter of the total 549,000 acres (220,000 ha) of cultivation area actually produces a yield, but irrigation and industrial processes mean that it delivers 70 percent of all wine production, albeit just simple, affordable wines.

Quality wines come from the areas near the almost 1,250-mile (2,000-km) coastline, which is lined with mountain chains. Where the mountainous barrier is broken

and the height of the land falls to below some 2,000 feet (600 m), fog and cool sea winds from the Pacific penetrate inland, moderating the sunlight and temperatures. The result is delayed ripening of the grapes and the development of more intense aromas. Without the protective shield of the mountains, conditions are too cold and moist for winegrowing.

SOUTH COAST

Vines were planted as early as 1820 by the San Juan Capistrano Mission on the South Coast of southern California. Today there are wineries from San Diego to Los Angeles, although most of the cultivation areas are found in Temecula and the San Pasqual Valley. Residual granite soils and locations at an altitude of about 1,650 feet (500 m) ensure convincing quality.

Winemakers achieve good results with Syrah and Tempranillo, as well as Chardonnay and Pinot Gris.

CENTRAL COAST

The American Viticultural Area of the Central Coast stretches from Santa Barbara to San Francisco, and includes 28 sub-AVAs. In Santa Barbara County, where more cool sea air penetrates the interior, wineries and winegrowers have specialized mainly on Chardonnay and Pinot Noir, producing some fabulous wines. Cabernet Sauvignon takes precedence over Merlot in San Luis Obispo County, although Syrah, Grenache, Viognier, and other varieties are cultivated with a similarly high level of success. The best known AVA is Paso Robles.

Monterey's vineyards extend over the dry Salinas Valley, where irrigation allows mainly Chardonnay to be produced, as well as Cabernet and Merlot in the warmer south. San Benito's hilly locations are attractive to specialist winemakers who are sparking interest with Pinot Noir and Chardonnay.

Monte Bello from Ridge Vineyards, Santa Cruz Mountains

Where it is cooler high up on the Santa Cruz Mountains, which extend as far as the coast, over 70 small craft wineries have been set up, while the most spectacular locations for superb Cabernets and Chardonnays are found high above Silicon Valley on the northeast side. Santa Clara Valley is also renowned for these varieties, while convincing white wines are the main focus in Livermore Valley near Oakland.

Renzoni Vineyards in the Temecula Valley on the South Coast

NORTH COAST

The Napa Valley and Sonoma, California's most famous cultivation regions, lie on the North Coast, north of San Francisco. This wine region also encompasses Mendocino County, where a quarter of what will soon be 17,300 acres (7,000 ha) under vine is now being farmed organically. It also includes Lake County further inland, along with Clear Lake AVA, where they have invested in many new facilities and are gaining a reputation for Cabernet Sauvignon and Sauvignon Blanc.

Sonoma

Built in 1823 and now carefully restored, the mission that was effectively the birthplace of Californian viticulture is located in the pleasant small town of Sonoma. With its gloriously wild coastline, Sonoma County consists of 13 clearly defined AVAs with different cultivation conditions. Locations nearer the coast, like Russian River Valley, are cooler and moister, and therefore attractive for growing Pinot Noir. Chardonnay, however, is the most widely cultivated variety. Where the climate is warmer, Cabernet Sauvignon dominates the red varieties and can produce great red wines, although excellent Syrahs and Zinfandels also ripen well under these conditions. The cool Carneros AVA, which lies next to San Pablo Bay and straddles parts of Sonoma and Napa Counties, is a stronghold of Pinot Noir and Chardonnay.

Crates full of Chardonnay grapes are transported in style on the Frei Ranch.

Sonoma offers a very wide range of microclimates and terroirs.

Napa Valley

The wines of the Napa Valley have made it one of the most prestigious and expensive wine regions in the world today, and the flagship of American viticulture in general. Enclosed by two mountain ranges, the valley runs in a north–south direction over 30 miles (50 km) or so. The locations become cooler the further south they are, due to the influence of San Pablo Bay. The ocean, which once covered the entire area, has left a wide range of extremely varied soil deposits, which is partly reflected in the 15 sub-AVAs.

Although there are excellent Chardonnays and Sauvignon Blancs, Napa's greatest and most famous wines are based on Cabernet Sauvignon, which can compete with the best *crus classés* from Bordeaux in complexity and aging potential, especially when they originate from the river terrace locations in Oakville and Rutherford. However, other AVAs are well known to aficionados for their varietal Cabernet Sauvignons or blends: Stag's Leap District, Mount Veeder, Diamond Mountain, and St Helena. Spring Mountain, Calistoga, and Howell Mountain are also famed for their impressive Zinfandels. Today Napa boasts over 400 wineries, which are often investing large sums in order to boost the quality and reputation of their wines.

Some locations in the Napa Valley often experience spring frosts. Wind turbines are used as a protective measure to keep the air circulating.

Codorníu Napa, the winery of the Spanish cava giant, was embedded perfectly into the Los Carneros landscape.

South America

Vine plots fit snugly into the terrain of Bodega Garzón in Maldonado province, Uruguay.

South America is well suited to winegrowing, especially on the slopes and foothills of the Andes—as the Spanish and Portuguese conquistadors realized centuries ago. Hernán Cortéz took the first Spanish graft cuttings to Mexico in 1522. During the 16th century the Jesuit missions were responsible for the spread of viticulture, but the next century saw wine production in Peru, Chile, and Argentina reach a level that became a thorn in the side of the conquering countries. But by then it was already too late—the tide could not be turned. With the development of global trade in the 19th century, French (and later other) premium grafts were introduced to Chile and Argentina from Europe, considerably boosting the

wine quality. Unfortunately, a large proportion of this heritage stock was pulled out as a result of the sales crisis during the 1960s. Barely 20 years later, a gradual upturn re-established Chile and Argentina within the ranks of the key wine-producing countries in the world.

PERU

Peru was the first country in South America to systematically cultivate vines. Back in the 16th century, some 99,000 acres (40,000 ha) were planted, the majority of which was destroyed by the phylloxera outbreak. A fresh start in the 1970s was hampered by the effects of the hot, arid climate. Although there are some high-quality wines, Muscat—the main grape grown—

is largely used to distil the national drink, *pisco*.

Small quantities of wine are also produced in Bolivia, Ecuador, Columbia, and Venezuela, often under tropical conditions that cause the inevitable associated problems. Where possible, cooler mountainous locations are preferred.

BRAZIL

Although the Portuguese introduced winegrowing in Brazil as early as 1532, it became more extensive only during the 1970s. From the mid-1980s great efforts were made to improve quality. Brazilian vintners made real advances only at the start of the new millennium with wines produced primarily from French varieties. Most of the wines come from Serra Gaúcha in Río Grande do Sul province in the south. The main development region in recent years has been Fronteira on the border with Uruguay.

URUGUAY

Uruguay stands out as different from other South American countries in terms of location and conditions. Its most important wine regions are around the capital, Montevideo, where the influence of the Atlantic Ocean and Rio de la Plata results in very well-balanced wines. The country's wine industry began to flourish in 1870, though the focus on high-quality wine production only began in the 1980s. Uruguay's *bodegas* have raised their profile mainly with red wines made from the Tannat grape.

Miolo's vineyards in the Vale dos Vinhedos, Brazil

Narbona winery near Carmelo, Uruguay

Argentina

With an output volume of around 409 million gallons (15.5 million hl), Argentina is the fifth largest producer in the world after France, Italy, Spain, and the USA. In recent years it has also managed to increase its exports, which look set to reach 95 million gallons (3.6 million hl). A series of events that began in the 1990s is responsible for this upturn. Given the strong Mediterranean influence on their culture, Argentinians had previously concentrated on producing simple table wine for the domestic market. Consumption of domestic wine went into a rapid decline as, amid a general economic boom, consumers turned to higher-quality imports. However, the industry underwent a gradual change in direction in the 1990s, with an emphasis on quality wines and hence increased exports. Malbec, the grape variety from Cahors in southwest France, developed intensely fruity aromas and velvety tex-

ture in Argentina's conditions; it provided the *bodegas* with the opportunity to break into the international market and attract attention with their appealing wines. The range of quality wines even stimulated fresh demand at home.

The most significant growing regions are in western Argentina, on the slopes of the Andes at altitudes of between approximately 980 and 5,900 feet (300–1,800 m).

The modern Bodega Dolium winery sits in the heart of its vineyards near Lúján de Cuyo in Mendoza.

Bodega Colomé in the Upper Calchaquí Valleys in Salta has the highest vineyards in the world, reaching up to some 10,200 feet (3,100 m).

These sandy, loamy soils are extremely dry, but they get enough irrigation thanks to an ingenious system of canals supplying water from the Andes. Mendoza is the most famous cultivation area. Its five different regions, which include the most famous and significant *bodegas*, produce two-thirds of all Argentinian wines, and the best ones into the bargain.

The warmer San Juan area supplies large quantities of cheap wine, while mostly full-bodied whites come from La Rioja, the cradle of viticulture in Argentina. Even farther to the north, vineyards have been planted in spectacular locations up to about 10,200 feet (3,100 m) above sea level, as at Cafayate and Salta. This is the source of the best white wines made from Torrentés, as well as some delightful red wines that are both balanced and fruity. Increasingly, the cool climate of southern Patagonia is attracting new investors, especially in the valleys of the Río Negro and Río Neuquén. In terms of fine wines, not only the white

and red French grape vines have been cultivated in Argentina, but also a large number of Spanish and Italian varieties— we have the cultural heritage of the country's immigrants to thank for that. So in second place to Malbec is Bonarda from northern Italy, which gives a pleasantly soft and fruity character to many cuvées. Such diverse varieties give Argentinian viticulture a promising future.

The architecture of Nieto Senetiner bodega reveals the Italian origins of its founders.

Mendoza is by far the most important cultivation region in Argentina. Its vast vineyards extend across the foothills of the Andes, which supply the region with essential water.

Chile

Spain's famous winemaker Miguel Torres called Chile "a viticultural paradise." As Chile was never ravaged by phylloxera, its vines remain ungrafted and the wines produced there are especially aromatic. What is more, other grape vine diseases rarely occur in the arid climate of the Central Valley, where the largest vineyards are found. Torres established a winery in Curicó in 1978. His modern approach to viticulture and cellar technology brought a fresh perspective to many traditional wine companies in Chile. For, although the country has a winegrowing tradition dating back to the 16th century, and despite all the European varieties introduced during the 19th, its wine industry found itself in crisis in the 1970s. The real upturn began only in the 1990s, when there were substantial (and sometimes foreign) investments and serious attempts to exploit the massive potential of the wine industry by planting premium varieties and installing the latest technology in wineries.

Other natural factors favor winegrowing in Chile. The wine regions in the east are bordered by the Andes and in the west by the Pacific. This geography gives temperatures that drop dramatically at night and can soar by day during the ripening season. This extends the growing period and produces intense aromas, in the case

One of Chile's oldest and largest wine companies is Viña San Pedro in the Curicó Valley.

Casablanca Valley in northern Chile was discovered as a wine region only in the 1980s. Today convincing wines flourish in a climate that is moderated by Pacific winds.

of red wines making them full-bodied with fine tannins.

The regions are subdivided according to the river valleys that run down to the ocean from the Andes and are provided with what is now a scientifically perfected irrigation system for the areas under vine. This gives the wineries the option of either producing pleasant everyday wines with high yields beyond Europe's wildest dreams, or growing grapes with excellent concentration by deliberately limiting yields. Chile, which produces around 277 million gallons (10.5 million hl) of wine each year, is equally successful on the export side. Its biggest cultivation regions in the Central Valley—Maipo, Rapel, Curicó, and Maule—yield impressive red wines, especially outstanding Cabernet Sauvignon, not to mention Merlot, Syrah, and Carmenère, the relative of Cabernet originally from Bordeaux, where it has all but disappeared. However, plenty of Chardonnay is produced here as well. Farther south, in Itata and Bío Bío, it is cooler and moister—in short, growing conditions are more difficult, but ideally suited nonetheless to Pinot Noir, Sauvignon Blanc, and Chardonnay. This also applies to the Casablanca and Aconcagua Valleys north of Santiago, or to the Elqui and Limarí Valleys, where other varieties such as Syrah and even Cabernet also produce very well-balanced, charming wines.

One of the great Chilean wines on the international market: Santa Rita

Casablanca Valley has made its name with fine Chardonnay, fresh Sauvignon Blanc, and elegant Pinot Noir.

The wine-producing countries | 207

Australia

The first grape vines may have been planted in the Governor's garden in Sydney as early as 1788, but it was the Gold Rush that gave a major boost to viticulture in Australia. It led in the mid-19th century to increased plantings in Victoria, which rose to become the main wine region on the mainland. As a result of the phylloxera disaster, it lost this position to South Australia, which had began to turn its land to good use and benefited from the influence of immigrants from Silesia, a longstanding winemaking region. The Barossa Valley became the hub of winemaking. It based its success on fortified sweet wines, which were in great demand within the Commonwealth.

The modern age dawned with the arrival of new immigrants in the 1950s, who wanted to drink dry wines. In order to meet this demand, they introduced new plantings of suitable grape varieties, and equipped wineries with stainless-steel tanks and temperature-control systems. Pioneering winemakers (such as Max Schubert, with his cult wine Grange) demonstrated how modern Australian wine should look and taste in the different growing regions. In this way, Shiraz and Cabernet Sauvignon from Down Under gained well-deserved recognition, as did its Merlot, Pinot Noir, Semillon, Sauvignon, Chardonnay, and Riesling.

For many years the warm regions of South Australia and New South Wales were the heartlands of wine production. However, other areas with cooler prevailing climates have become increasingly

Lush vegetation on the Margaret River

significant in the course of the last two or three decades. Some have long since carved out a reputation as a source of quality wines, including McLaren Vale, Clare Valley, and Eden Valley, as well as growing areas in Victoria and Tasmania, which is especially cool. Suitable conditions are even found in South Australia, on the Limestone Coast near Wrattonbully, for instance. The net result is that the overall range of Australian wines has become considerably more diverse and exciting.

Australia may have over 2,000 wineries, but for the most part farmers supply the grapes while 80 percent of wine production and sales is in the hands of large-scale companies. Vineyards have been extended substantially to cope with a sharp increase in demand. Between 1998 and 2011 alone, the areas dedicated to winegrowing have increased from some 304,000 to 388,000 acres (123,000–157,000 ha). Drought and severe weather conditions have meant that the 2004/2005 production record of over 370 million gallons (14 million hl) of wine remained unbeaten in 2011, and the volume that year was even down by around 80 millions gallons (3 million hl). There is far greater potential, however, when natural conditions are favorable. Unfortunately, the market has not kept pace in recent years, and grape farmers now find themselves facing sales problems.

Horizontal rotary tanks and computerized temperature-controlled fermentation tanks: As is the case throughout Australia, Haselgrove winery in McLaren Vale relies on state-of-the-art technology.

Premium varieties are not a recent phenomenon in Australia: The image shows a hundred-year-old Shiraz vine stock.

In traditional winegrowing countries, the character of the wine is primarily defined by the prevailing natural conditions in the vineyard. As immigrants, Australian winemakers brought clear ideas of how their wine should taste from their native lands, and set out on a new course that is still successful today—the blending of grapes from many different sources. It goes without saying that grapes can be grown only in regions offering the right conditions, which are now successfully met in over 60 regions and 103 specified designations of origin in Australia.

Most of the grapes are produced in Lower Murray, Big Rivers, and North-West Victoria, in very warm regions where the vineyards can be irrigated by the Murray, Darling, and Murrumbidgee Rivers. Quality wine production, however, mainly requires areas where temperatures are more moderate during the maturation period.

Domaine Chandon in the cool Yarra Valley

NEW SOUTH WALES

The best-known wine region in New South Wales is the hot, humid Hunter Valley, to the north of Sydney. Despite difficult conditions, 154 wineries produce very convincing wines made mostly from Shiraz and Cabernet Sauvignon for reds, and from Semillon and Chardonnay for whites. This also applies to the companies in Mudgee on the western slopes of the Great Dividing Range. Its cool climate and elegant wines make Orange, a city west of Sydney, a rapidly growing cultivation region.

Vines and irrigation tanks in Hunter Valley

VICTORIA

The cooler climate of Victoria's regions in and around Melbourne—Yarra Valley, Geelong, and the Mornington Peninsula in the Bass Strait—means they are particularly well suited to Chardonnay, Pinot Noir, and, to some extent, Bordeaux blends. Intriguing fortified Muscat wines continue to be produced in Rutherglen and Glenrowan in the northeast, while the cooler regions of the Pyrenees and Macedon Ranges are experiencing an upturn.

Margaret River in West Australia: great wines and a fascinating natural setting

SOUTH AND WESTERN AUSTRALIA

Barossa in South Australia is the heartland of big, full-bodied Shiraz, while Clare Valley north of Adelaide is famed for its dry Rieslings, as is Eden Valley, where fabulous

Clare Valley, famed for Riesling

Shiraz wines are also produced. Shiraz also thrives on the Limestone Coast, although Chardonnay is the dominant grape there, while Coonawarra with its premium terra rossa soils is mainly famous for Cabernet. In Western Australia, in the Margaret River's famous growing region, as well as in the southern areas of Pemberton and

Great Southern near the coast, the excellent climatic conditions yield very well-balanced, elegant white and red wines.

TASMANIA

The cooler climate of the island of Tasmania is an attractive option for winemakers: Ideally suited to sparkling wines, it also produces good Rieslings, Gewürztraminer, and Pinot Gris. Some inspired Pinot Noir comes from the beautiful, warmer Tamar Valley.

Cool beauty: the Tamar Valley on Tasmania

New Zealand

Although the missionary Samuel Marsden introduced grape vines to New Zealand as early as 1819, modern viticulture began to develop in the country only during the 1960s. Initially, the focus was on the warmer, almost subtropical regions of the North Island, such as Northland and Auckland, while the more southerly areas and the South Island were considered too cold. Dramatic changes were made during the 1980s, however, when the areas under vine increased from a good 9,900 acres (4,000 ha) in 1989 to today's total of almost 74,000 acres (30,000 ha).

New Zealand's success as a wine nation is associated with its winemakers' realization that the cool climate of its southern regions was actually perfectly suited to the cultivation of Sauvignon Blanc. Beautifully fresh on the palate, its typical vegetal aromas redolent of asparagus and beans, combined with citrus fruits, mango, and passion fruit, have made it the country's flagship wine and a resounding export success. It now occupies a cultivation area of 35,000 acres (14,000 ha). Müller-Thurgau, an inconsequential grape of the 1970s, is out of the picture, but remarkable quality has been achieved with Chardonnay, Riesling, Pinot Gris, and Gewürztraminer.

With its maritime climate and ancient soils, Waiheke Island off Auckland is particularly suited to Bordeaux varieties.

The palm trees in Hawke's Bay are indicative of the heat that ripens New Zealand's top Cabernets in this region.

As far as red wines are concerned, a few good ones still come from north Waiheke Island, but Hawke's Bay, with its gravelly soils, has proved the best source of Bordeaux-style blends. Today Pinot Noir has turned out to be New Zealand's second trump card, overtaking even the popular Chardonnay's 9,590 acres (3,880 ha), with 11,490 acres (4,650 ha) under vine. Wairarapa, with Martinborough district at the southern tip of the North Island, stands out as an excellent area for Pinot Noir, though very aromatic white wines are produced here as well.

The best-known and most important source of Sauvignon is Marlborough in the north of the South Island, where this variety grows on flat, rather infertile alluvial soils in a region heavily influenced by the sea. The *terroir* in neighboring Nelson is similar, though it has higher rainfall. Canterbury, which was previously considered too cold for viticulture, lies on the east coast, where very fresh, vibrant white wines are now emerging from Christchurch on the hills near Waipara and the Banks Peninsula. Even the intensely aromatic Pinot Noir from this region is impressive.

Central Otago, the most southerly wine-growing region in the world, is experiencing a major upturn. Its imposing vineyards are located on the spectacular lakesides of New Zealand's Southern Alps. Despite a climate that actually defies all the current ideas about winemaking, the Chardonnay and Pinot Noir grapes from this region produce wines of great finesse.

Island-produced red wines: Goldwater Estate on Waiheke

Hawke's Bay is also famous for its rich Chardonnays.

Glossary

A

acids These give the wine vitality and prolong its freshness; however, the acidity must be balanced.

Appellation d'Origine Protégée (AOP) Protected designation of origin for French wines (formerly AOC).

assemblage Blend of high-quality wines (cuvée); coupage, on the other hand, is a blend of low-quality wines.

American Viticultural Area (AVA) Protected designation of origin for American wines, equivalent to French appellations.

B

barrique Small oak cask with a capacity of 225 liters (59 US gallons), used in the maturation of red wines in many countries, as well as for fermentation and maturation of white wines.

blend Mixture of different varieties of grapes or wines to enhance the positive qualities of the individual components; standard practice in branded wines to ensure consistent quality for each vintage.

Botrytis cinerea Noble rot affecting grapes, producing distinctive aromas and flavors.

bottle maturity The point at which a wine is fully developed and ready for bottling; also describes the aging of a wine in the bottle.

C

cap As red wine ferments, a layer of grape skins and other solids float to the surface of the container; this must be "punched down" and mixed in with the must to release color pigments, aromatic substances, and tannins.

carbon dioxide (CO_2) A natural gas and a by-product of alcoholic fermentation.

cava Type of Spanish sparkling wine, made using the traditional bottle fermentation method.

cellar bottled Wines made from grapes that were not grown or developed by the bottler.

chaptalization (enrichment) Addition of sugar before fermentation to increase the alcohol content; not permitted for every wine.

clarification Natural, gentle process allowing unwanted solid matter in the must or wine to sink slowly to the bottom of the container.

clone Vines propagated from a genetically identical mother plant.

clos Term used in Burgundy for a vineyard enclosed by a wall or hedge.

cork taste Where wine becomes impaired by faulty corks, mainly through the formation of the chemical compound 2,4,6-Trichloroanisole (TCA), which is caused by mildew. Also known as cork taint.

coulure Where grapes fall off after flowering due to a metabolic deficiency in the vine.

cru Literally "growth"; used in the wider sense for an excellent location, or the wine from this area.

cuvée Blend of high-quality wines, assemblage; used in sparkling wine production to describe the free-run juice from the pressing.

D

dégustation French term for wine tasting.

Denominação de Origem Controlada (DOC) Controlled designation of origin for Portuguese quality wines.

Denominación de Origen (DO) Controlled designation of origin for Spanish quality wines.

Denominazione di Origine Controllata (DOC) Controlled designation of origin for Italian quality wines.

deposit Lees or sediment.

de-stem To remove the grapes from stems before fermentation; to machine-process.

domaine French term for wine estate.

E

enology The science of winemaking.

Erzeugerabfüllung "Estate-bottled" — German term for wines made from grapes grown on the estate named on the label, also applies to cooperative wines.

extract All the nonvolatile substances present in wine: acids, minerals, sugar, phenols, glycerin.

F

fermentation Process in wine production during which sugar is converted into alcohol and carbon dioxide, and the must turns into wine.

filtration Fast technique for separating solids from the wine using filters; its use in high-quality wine is controversial, as it can result in loss of color and valuable substances.

fining Clarification of the wine, helping to stabilize it; a fining agent is added to the wine to bind the unwanted cloudy particles, which then settle as sediment.

fortified wines Port, Sherry, Madeira, Malaga, Marsala, Banyuls, and Rivesaltes, among others.

fortify To add alcohol in order to stop fermentation and increase the alcohol content of the wines.

full fermentation All the sugar is converted into alcohol; the wine has little or only minimal residual sweetness.

G

grand cru Literally "great growth" — classification for the top locations in Burgundy and Alsace, and general term for outstanding wine.

H

hybrid grapevine Offspring of two grape varieties that do not belong to the same species (also known as an interspecific cross); the aim is to combine the positive qualities of different species in one variety.

I

Indication Géographique Protégée (IGP) French country wine category (formerly Vin de Pays).

Indicazione Geografica Tipica (IGT) Italian country wine category.

integrated viticulture Cultivation method that avoids the use of pesticides in order to protect beneficial organisms and the environment.

L

land consolidation (re-parceling) Measure taken in mid-20th century to remodel over half of the cultivation area in West Germany, in order to improve the viticulture.

M

mash Lightly crushed grapes that are transferred to the fermentation tanks with the must; red wines are fermented on the mash.

mash heating The mash is heated to release pigments from the skins.

malolactic fermentation Conversion of malic acid into lactic acid by bacteria in order to reduce the acidity of the wine. Also known as malolactic conversion.

mass selection Process in which the best vines in a vineyard are selected; compare clonal selection, in which a single clone is reproduced with a genetically identical structure.

maturation All the processes that take place in the winery after fermentation is completed and develop the wine before bottling.

minerality Special taste, often slightly salty.

must Unfermented grape juice.

must weight Determines the ripeness level of grapes, measured according to different scales: Brix (USA), Baumé (France and most of Europe), Oechsle (Germany).

mutage Where fermentation is stopped by adding alcohol or sulfur dioxide.

N

noble rot See: *Botrytis cinerea*.

O

Oechsle Measurement based on specific gravity of must, named for German physicist Ferdinand Oechsle. A must with a specific gravity of 1.09 measures 90 °Oe. This scale is used in Germany and Switzerland.

organoleptic assessment Test of wine quality by appearance, smell, and taste.

oxidation Chemical reaction caused by overexposure of the wine to oxygen; the wine becomes stale, and changes color; this can occur in the bottle, or even in the cask or must.

P

pH level Measurement for the degree of acidity in a wine; the lower the pH level, the more acidic the wine tastes; 7 is neutral (as in pure water).

pigeage In red wine fermentation, the process of "punching" the cap regularly; traditionally used in Pinot Noir, and now in many other top wines as well.

polyphenols Chemical component in wine found in color pigments, tannins, and flavoring; has beneficial effects for the human body.

pomace Mass of grape solids that are left after pressing (white wines) or after fermentation (red wines); may be distilled to make brandy.

press To extract grape juice before fermentation.

pruning Radically cutting back the plant's shoots to promote vine growth and enhance quality.

pumping over Process in fermentation of red wine to keep the cap submerged in the must, so that as many pigments and aromas as possible are released from the skins. In French: *remontage*.

Q

quality wine (or fine wine) General term for high-quality wines with designations of origin, as opposed to simple table wines.

quinta Portuguese winery or wine estate, comparable to the French *château*.

R

racking Process of pumping over clarified wine into an empty container to remove unwanted lees.

reduction Opposite of oxidation; chemical reaction that takes place in airtight conditions; reductive wines are extremely fresh and aromatic.

residual sweetness Sugar that has not been converted into alcohol during fermentation gives a wine its natural residual sweetness.

rootstock Vine cutting used to graft a different vine species.

S

selected yeast Cultured yeast that is used in fermentation to convert the must into wine; reactions tend to be more predictable than those of natural yeasts found on the grapes themselves, which can prove problematic.

solera System for producing fortified wines, especially Sherry and Madeira; the aim is to maintain the same quality standard each year.

sommelier, sommelière French term for a male/female wine steward.

stabilization Stage reached when all unwanted and suspended particles and cloudiness have been removed from a wine (e.g. through fining); the wine in the bottle has a clear appearance and does not form any gases.

sulfur Used extensively in winemaking; from protecting the vines to sterilization of wooden casks and preservation of the wine.

T

tannins Substances in wine with an astringent effect, important for aging of red wines; very pronounced in young reds, they do, however, soften as the wine matures.

tartrates Crystals that settle at the bottom of a wine bottle. They are formed when acids break down in wine; they do not impair the quality of the wine, however, so complaints are unwarranted!

typicity The classic expression of a wine, especially as relates to a specific *terroir*; its distinctive character that comes from the location in which the grapes are grown.

V

vegetal Wines with immature, green notes, caused by grapes that have not fully ripened.

Verband Deutscher Prädikatsweingüter (VDP) Protected designation and abbreviation for the association of around 200 wine estates in Germany.

vine training systems Various methods for pruning and training vine shoots. They ensure that the shoots and foliage do not trail on the soil, and that the ventilation of the vines is better, thus making them less susceptible to fungal infections. The main systems used are Gobelet, and single and double Guyot.

vinification Winemaking, from the point at which the grapes are delivered to the winery until the wine is bottled.

vintage Year in which the grapes for a wine are grown; also generally refers to the characteristics of a particular harvest in terms of the weather and growth cycle of the grapes. French: *millésime*.

Vitis Plant genus that also includes the grape vine; the most important species is *Vitis vinifera*, which comprises some 8,000 varieties.

W

winemaker Vintners, especially in New World regions, who have often been trained in cellar technology; also the person responsible for the wine in a company.

wine cooperative Association of winegrowers who collaborate in the production and marketing of the wine of individual members.

Y

yeast Microorganisms, some of which can produce fermentation in grape juice. *See also*: selected yeasts.

yield Grape crop size; measured in hectoliters per hectare (hl/ha) in Europe and tons per acre (TPA) in most of the New World.

Index

H

harvesting 68ff., 74
Harz 153
Hawke's Bay 213
herbicide 43, 53
Hessische Bergstraße 151
Hong Kong 188
horn dung 48
Hungary 176

I

icewine 67
IGP 131, 137
India190
insecticide 43, 53
integrated production 44f.
Israel 183
Italy 138ff.

J

Japan 129, 191
Jerez 163
Johannisberg 148
Jura 133
Jurançon 135

K

Kazakhstan 191
Klein Karoo 187
Kremstal 158
Kvevris 179
Kyrgyzstan 191

L

lactic acid 101
ladybugs 49
Lake Geneva 156
Lake Neusiedl 158, 160

Langhe 141
Languedoc 137
Lazio 145
Lebanon 182f.
Leithaberg 160
Les Baux de Provence 136
Levante 166
limestone 37
Limestone Coast 211
Limousin 108, 109
Loire 129, 134
Lombardy 141
Loreley 150
Lower Murray 210
Luxemburg 154f.

M

Macedonia 181
maceration 17
Madeira 135, 168
Madrid 166
mash 17, 97, 98, 100
macrofauna 33
Málaga 163, 167
Malbec 30
malic acid 101
malolactic fermentation 99, 101
Malta 182
Malvasia 21, 168
Marche, the 145
Marcillac 135
Marlborough 213
Marsala 147
Marseille 130
maturation 78
Maury 137
McLaren Vale 209
mechanization 40f.
Mediterranean 129, 180ff.
Médoc 135
Mendoza 205

Merlot 19, 135, 142, 143, 144, 147, 153, 155, 157, 159, 160, 161, 166, 167, 178, 180, 185, 193, 194, 196, 199, 207, 208
Merrandier 106
Michigan 195
microclimate 35, 80
microflora 32
microorganisms 32
Middle Rhine 150
mildew 43, 46, 54, 56
Minervois 137
Moldova 179
Monastrell 30
Monferrato 141
Montenegro 181
Monterey 199
Morat 156
Morocco 183
Moscato 21, 141
Mosel 148, 150
Müller-Thurgau 21
Murcia 167
Muscat 21, 132, 136, 137, 169, 186, 203, 210
Muscat de Rivesaltes 137
must 83, 84, 92, 96, 103, 104
must weight scales 82

N

Nahe 151
Napa Valley 201
Naples 147
Narbonne 130
Nebbiolo 30
Nematodes 54
Nero d'Avola 147
Neuchâtel 156
New Mexico 192

Picture credits

All photographs: © Armin Faber and
    Thomas Pothmann, Düsseldorf

With the exception of:
© www.beerfoto.com: 112, 113
© Ben-Joseph, Michael, Herzliya: 183
    b.r.
© Budd, Jim, London: 193
© Chateau Mercian: 191
© Chien, Mark. L.: 194 t.
© Doluca: 182 l.
© Dominé, André: 12, 16, 24 r., 34 b.,
    36 l., 42/43 b., 133 r., 136 t.r.,
    137 b.r., 167 b.r., 183 l., 184, 185,
    186, 187, 199 t.r., 202, 203 r.
© Hochschule Geisenheim University /
    Photo: Dr. B. Berkelmann: 55 / Photo:
    Prof. H. Holst: 56 t., 57 t., 54 t., 56
    b., 57 b., 58 / Photo: B. Loskill: 54 t.
    / Diagram: B. Loskill: 59

© Gallo: 200 t.
© h.f.ullmann publishing GmbH / Photo:
    Food-Foto-Köln: 179 t. / Photo: Ellen
    Thießen: 8
© ICEX, Madrid / Photo: C. Navajas:
    31 b. / Photo: I. Muñoz-Seca: 20 t. /
    Photo: C. Tejero: 23 b.
© KEO pic. Limassol, Cyprus: 182 r.
© KOJ Kôshû of Japan: 190 b.
© Miolo Wine Group: 203 l.
© Randall Tagg Photography/New York
    Wine & Grape Foundation: 194 b.
© Sadler, Steve: 195
© Seguin Moreau, Cognac: 111
© Südtiroler Weinwerbung: 20 b.
© Temecula Valley Winegrowers Associa-
    tion, Leigh Castelli: 199 b.
© Wilson, Woodrow: 190 t

Book@
Book+@-book
in one

A Wine Lover's Guide (GB)

JUST FOLLOW THESE EASY STEPS:

❶ There is a download code to be found at the bottom of this page.

❷ Go to www.ullmann-publishing.com/en and click on "book + e-book."

❸ Enter your email address and the download code.

❹ The download link will be sent to your email account; then you can download the eBook as ePUB and transfer it to your tablet pc or reader.

Your personal E-Book-Code

36Q1 G7JN 5C0K G5DS